CAMBRIDGE LIBRARY COLLECTION

Books of enduring scholarly value

Religion

For centuries, scripture and theology were the focus of prodigious amounts
of scholarship and publishing, dominated in the English-speaking world
by the work of Protestant Christians. Enlightenment philosophy and
science, anthropology, ethnology and the colonial experience all brought
new perspectives, lively debates and heated controversies to the study of
religion and its role in the world, many of which continue to this day. This
series explores the editing and interpretation of religious texts, the history of
religious ideas and institutions, and not least the encounter between religion
and science.

The Christian Ecclesia

This is one of the best-known works of Fenton Hort (1828–1892), Professor
of Divinity at Cambridge. Compiled in 1897, it is a posthumous collection
of a series of lectures delivered by Hort in 1888 and 1889, covering the
origins and development of the early Church. Starting with a discussion
on the meaning of 'ecclesia', Hort traces church history from the New
Testament accounts of the Last Supper and the Resurrection to the problems
Christianity faced in the second century. Hort conveys his meaning with
absolute clarity, taking a scrupulous, almost scientific approach in his
consideration of literary evidence. Four of his sermons are also included,
and the book itself stands as a record of the last words spoken in public by
Hort. The Christian Ecclesia provides a fascinating account of the beginnings
of Christianity and is one of the most significant works by this prolific
nineteenth-century theologian.

Cambridge University Press has long been a pioneer in the reissuing of out-of-print titles from its own backlist, producing digital reprints of books that are still sought after by scholars and students but could not be reprinted economically using traditional technology. The Cambridge Library Collection extends this activity to a wider range of books which are still of importance to researchers and professionals, either for the source material they contain, or as landmarks in the history of their academic discipline.

Drawing from the world-renowned collections in the Cambridge University Library, and guided by the advice of experts in each subject area, Cambridge University Press is using state-of-the-art scanning machines in its own Printing House to capture the content of each book selected for inclusion. The files are processed to give a consistently clear, crisp image, and the books finished to the high quality standard for which the Press is recognised around the world. The latest print-on-demand technology ensures that the books will remain available indefinitely, and that orders for single or multiple copies can quickly be supplied.

The Cambridge Library Collection will bring back to life books of enduring scholarly value (including out-of-copyright works originally issued by other publishers) across a wide range of disciplines in the humanities and social sciences and in science and technology.

The Christian Ecclesia

*A Course of Lectures on the Early History and
Early Conceptions of the Ecclesia, and Four
Sermons*

FENTON JOHN ANTHONY HORT

CAMBRIDGE
UNIVERSITY PRESS

CAMBRIDGE UNIVERSITY PRESS

Cambridge, New York, Melbourne, Madrid, Cape Town, Singapore,
São Paolo, Delhi, Dubai, Tokyo

Published in the United States of America by Cambridge University Press, New York

www.cambridge.org
Information on this title: www.cambridge.org/9781108007559

© in this compilation Cambridge University Press 2009

This edition first published 1897
This digitally printed version 2009

ISBN 978-1-108-00755-9 Paperback

THE

CHRISTIAN ECCLESIA

THE
CHRISTIAN ECCLESIA

A COURSE OF LECTURES

ON THE EARLY HISTORY AND EARLY CONCEPTIONS OF THE ECCLESIA

AND FOUR SERMONS

BY

FENTON JOHN ANTHONY HORT D.D.
LADY MARGARET'S READER IN DIVINITY IN THE
UNIVERSITY OF CAMBRIDGE

London
MACMILLAN AND CO., LIMITED
NEW YORK: THE MACMILLAN COMPANY
1897

PREFACE.

THIS book consists in the first place of a course of lectures delivered by Dr Hort as Lady Margaret Professor in the Michaelmas Terms of 1888 and 1889 on 'The Early History and the Early Conceptions of the Christian Ecclesia'. The plan of the lectures is the same as that of the Lectures on Judaistic Christianity.

They contain a careful survey of the evidence to be derived from the literature of the Apostolic age for the solution of a fundamental problem.

The title 'Ecclesia' was chosen, as the opening lecture explains, expressly for its freedom from the distracting associations which have gathered round its more familiar synonyms. It is in itself a sufficient indication of the spirit of genuine historical enquiry in which the study was undertaken.

The original scheme included an investigation into the evidence of the early Christian centuries, and the book is therefore in one sense no doubt incomplete. On

the other hand it is no mere fragment. The lectures
as they stand practically exhaust the evidence of the
New Testament, at least as far as the Early History
of Christian institutions is concerned. And Dr Hort's
conclusions on the vexed questions with regard to
the 'Origines' of the different Orders in the Christian
Ministry will no doubt be scanned with peculiar
interest. It is however by no means too much to say
that it was the other side of his subject, 'the Early
Conceptions of the Ecclesia', that gave it its chief
attraction for Dr Hort. And on this side unfortunately
the limitations of lecturing compelled him to leave
many things unsaid to which he attached the greatest
importance.

An effort has been made to supply this deficiency
by including in the volume four Sermons dealing
with different applications of the fundamental conception preached on different occasions during the
last twenty years of his life. Two of these Dr Hort
at one time intended to incorporate in the same
volume with his Hulsean Lectures '*The Way, The
Truth, The Life*'. The other two were printed by
request directly after they had been delivered. The
last has a special interest as the last public utterance
of its author. It is the expression in a concentrated
form of the thought of a lifetime on the vital conditions of Church life in special relation to the pressing
needs of to-day.

The course in 1889 began with a somewhat full

recapitulation of the course delivered in 1888. I have not thought it worth while to print this recapitulation at length. A few modifications have however been introduced from it into the text of the original lectures, and a few additions appended as footnotes. Otherwise the Lectures are printed, with a few necessary verbal alterations, as they stand in the Author's MSS. I am further responsible for the divisions of the text, for the titles of the Lectures, and for the headings of the separate paragraphs.

My best thanks are due to the Rev. F. G. Masters, formerly scholar of Corpus Christi College, Cambridge, for much help in revising the proof-sheets and for the compilation of the index.

J. O. F. MURRAY.

EMMANUEL COLLEGE, CAMBRIDGE.
March 12th, 1897.

CONTENTS.

LECTURES ON THE EARLY HISTORY AND THE
EARLY CONCEPTIONS OF THE ECCLESIA.

I.

THE WORD ECCLESIA.

II.

THE APOSTLES IN RELATION TO THE ECCLESIA.

III.

EARLY STAGES IN THE GROWTH OF THE ECCLESIA.

XIII.

Brief Notes on various Epistles, and Recapitulation.

FOUR SERMONS.

LECTURE I.

THE WORD ECCLESIA.

THE subject on which I propose to lecture this term is *The early conceptions and early history of the Christian Ecclesia.* The reason why I have chosen the term Ecclesia is simply to avoid ambiguity. The English term *church,* now the most familiar representative of *ecclesia* to most of us, carries with it associations derived from the institutions and doctrines of later times, and thus cannot at present without a constant mental effort be made to convey the full and exact force which originally belonged to *ecclesia.* There would moreover be a second ambiguity in the phrase *the early history of the Christian Church* arising out of the vague comprehensiveness with which the phrase ' History of the Church' is conventionally employed.

It would of course have been possible to have recourse to a second English rendering 'congregation', which has the advantage of suggesting some of those

elements of meaning which are least forcibly suggested by the word 'church' according to our present
use. 'Congregation' was the only rendering of ἐκκλησία
in the English New Testament as it stood throughout
Henry VIII.'s reign, the substitution of 'church'
being due to the Genevan revisers; and it held its
ground in the Bishops' Bible in no less primary a
passage than Matt. xvi. 18 till the Jacobean revision
of 1611, which we call the Authorized Version. But
'congregation' has disturbing associations of its own
which render it unsuitable for our special purpose;
and moreover its use in what might seem a rivalry to
so venerable, and rightly venerable, a word as
'church' would be only a hindrance in the way of
recovering for 'church' the full breadth of its
meaning. 'Ecclesia' is the only perfectly colourless
word within our reach, carrying us back to the
beginnings of Christian history, and enabling us in
some degree to get behind words and names to the
simple facts which they originally denoted.

The larger part of our subject lies in the region of
what we commonly call Church History; the general
Christian history of the ages subsequent to the
Apostolic age. But before entering on that region
we must devote some little time to matter contained
in the Bible itself. It is hopeless to try to understand either the actual Ecclesia of post-apostolic
times, or the thoughts of its own contemporaries
about it, without first gaining some clear impressions

as to the Ecclesia of the Apostles out of which it grew; to say nothing of the influence exerted all along by the words of the apostolic writings, and by other parts of Scripture. And again the Ecclesia of the Apostles has likewise antecedents which must not be neglected, immediately in facts and words recorded by the Evangelists, and ultimately in the institutions and teaching of the Old Covenant.

In this preliminary part of our subject, to say the least, we shall find it convenient to follow the order of time.

I am sorry to be unable to recommend any books as sufficiently coinciding with our subject generally. Multitudes of books in all civilised languages bear directly or indirectly upon parts of it: but I doubt whether it would be of any real use to attempt a selection. In the latter part of the subject we come on ground which has been to a certain extent worked at by several German writers within the last few years, and I may have occasion from time to time to refer to some of them: they may however be passed over for the present.

The sense of the word in the Old Testament.

The Ecclesia of the New Testament takes its name and primary idea from the Ecclesia of the Old Testament. What then is the precise meaning of the term Ecclesia as we find it in the Old Testament?

The word itself is a common one in classical Greek

and was adopted by the LXX. translators from Deuteronomy onwards (*not* in the earlier books of the Pentateuch) as their usual rendering of *qāhāl.*

Two important words are used in the Old Testament for the gathering together of the people of Israel, or their representative heads, *'ēdhāh* [R.V. congregation] and *qāhāl* [R.V. assembly].

Συναγωγή [*Synagogè*] is the usual, almost the universal, LXX. rendering of *'ēdhāh*, as also in the earlier books of the Pentateuch of *qāhāl.* So closely connected in original use are the two terms Synagogue and Ecclesia, which afterwards came to be fixed in deep antagonism !

Neither of the two Hebrew terms was strictly technical : both were at times applied to very different kinds of gatherings from the gatherings of the people, though *qāhāl* had always a *human* reference of some sort, gatherings of individual men or gatherings of nations. The two words were so far coincident in meaning that in many cases they might apparently be used indifferently : but in the first instance they were not strictly synonymous. *'ēdhāh* (derived from a root *y'dh* used in the Niphal in the sense of gathering together, specially gathering together by appointment or agreement) is properly, when applied to Israel, the society itself, formed by the children of Israel or their representative heads, whether assembled or not assembled.

On the other hand *qāhāl* is properly their actual

meeting together: hence we have a few times the phrase *qᵉhăl 'ēdhāh* 'the assembly of the congregation' (rendered by the LXX. translators in Ex. xii. 6 πᾶν τὸ πλῆθος συναγωγῆς υἱῶν Ἰσραήλ, in Num. xiv. 5 where no equivalent is given for *qᵉhăl* πάσης συνάγωγῆς υἱῶν Ἰσραήλ) and also *qᵉhăl 'ăm* 'the assembly of the people' (rendered in Judg. xx. 2 ἐν ἐκκλησίᾳ τοῦ λαοῦ τοῦ θεοῦ, in Jer. xxvi. (LXX. xxxiii.) 17 πάσῃ τῇ συναγωγῇ τοῦ λαοῦ). The special interest of this distinction lies in its accounting for the choice of the rendering ἐκκλησία: *qāhāl* is derived from an obsolete root meaning to call or summon, and the resemblance to the Greek καλέω naturally suggested to the LXX. translators the word ἐκκλησία, derived from καλέω (or rather ἐκκαλέω) in precisely the same sense.

There is no foundation for the widely spread notion that ἐκκλησία means a people or a number of individual men *called out* of the world or mankind. In itself the idea is of course entirely Scriptural, and moreover it is associated with the word and idea 'called,' 'calling,' 'call.' But the compound verb ἐκκαλέω is never so used, and ἐκκλησία never occurs in a context which suggests this supposed sense to have been present to the writer's mind. Again, it would not have been unnatural if this sense of *calling out* from a larger body had been as it were put into the word in later times, when it had acquired religious associations. But as a matter of fact we do not find that it was so. The original *calling out* is simply the calling of the

citizens of a Greek town out of their houses by the
herald's trumpet to summon them to the assembly
and Numb. x. shews that the summons to the Jewish
assembly was made in the same way. In the actual
usage of both *qāhāl* and ἐκκλησία this primary idea of
summoning is hardly to be felt. They mean simply
an assembly of the people; and accordingly in the
Revised Version of the Old Testament 'assembly' is
the predominant rendering of *qāhāl.*

So much for the original and distinctive force of
the two words, in Hebrew and Greek. Now we must
look a little at their historical application in the Old
Testament.

'*ēdhāh* is by far the commoner word of the two
in Exodus, Leviticus, Numbers and Joshua, but it is
wholly absent from Deuteronomy. The two words
are used in what appears to be practically the same
sense in successive clauses of Lev. iv. 13 ; Num. xvi.
3 ; and they are coupled together, ἐν μέσῳ ἐκκλησίας
καὶ συναγωγῆς, in Prov. v. 14 (LXX.). Both alike are described sometimes as the congregation or assembly of
Israel, sometimes as the congregation or assembly of
Jehovah ; sometimes as the congregation or the
assembly absolutely. In the later books '*ēdhāh* goes
almost out of use. It is absent from Chronicles except once in an extract from Kings or the source of
Kings (2 Chr. v. 6). It recurs (in the sense of congregation of Israel, I mean) but two or three times in
the Psalms and the same in the Prophets.

In these, and in the poetical books, *qāhāl* is hardly more common, but it abounds in Chronicles, Ezra and Nehemiah. It would seem that after the return from the Exile this, the more definite and formal word, came to combine the shades of meaning belonging to both. Thus ἐκκλησία, as the primary Greek representative of *qāhāl* would naturally for Greek-speaking Jews mean the congregation of Israel quite as much as an assembly of the congregation.

In the Apocrypha both συναγωγή and ἐκκλησία are to be found : but it would take too long to ex-amine the somewhat intricate variations of sense to be found there[1]. But with regard to these words, like many others of equal importance, there is a great gap, in our knowledge of the usage of Greek Judaism. Philo gives us no help, the thoughts which connect themselves with the idea of a national ἐκ-κλησία being just of the kind which had least interest for him; and Josephus's ostentatious classicalism de-prives us of the information which a better Jew in his position might have afforded us. For our purpose it would be of peculiar interest to know what and how much the term ἐκκλησία meant to Jews of the Dispersion at the time of the Christian Era : but here again we are, I fear, wholly in the dark.

---

[1] There is an indication that συναγωγή was coming to mean the local congregation in Sir. xxiv. 23 and especially in Ps. Sal. x. 7. 8.

The sense of the word in the Gospels.

It is now time to come to the New Testament and its use of ἐκκλησία, bearing in mind that it is a word which had already a history of its own, and which was associated with the whole history of Israel. It is also well to remember that its antecedents, as it was used by our Lord and His Apostles, are of two kinds, derived from the past and the present respectively. Part, the most important part, of its meaning came from its ancient and what we may call its religious use, that is from the sense or senses which it had borne in the Jewish Scriptures; part also of its meaning could not but come from the senses in which it was still current in the everyday life of Jews. We may be able to obtain but little independent evidence on this last head: but it needs only a little reflexion to feel sure that in this as in other cases contemporary usage cannot have been wholly inoperative.

The actual word ἐκκλησία, as many know, is in the Gospels confined to two passages of St Matthew. This fact has not unnaturally given rise to doubts as to the trustworthiness of the record. These doubts however seem to me to be in reality unfounded. If indeed it were true that matter found in a single Gospel only is to be regarded with suspicion as not proceeding from fundamental documents common to more than one, then doubtless these passages would be open to doubt. But if, as I believe to be the true view, each evangelist had independent knowledge or had access to fresh materials by which he was able to make trustworthy additions to that which he obtained from previous records, then there is no *a priori* reason for suspecting these two passages of the First Gospel.

It is further urged that these passages have the appearance of having been thrust into the text in the Second Century in order to support the growing authority of the Ecclesia as an external power. An interpolation of the supposed kind would however be unexampled, and there is nothing in the passages themselves, when carefully read, which bears out the suggestion. Nay, the manner in which St Peter's name enters into the language about the building of Messiah's Ecclesia could not be produced by any view respecting his office which was current in the Second Century. In truth, the application of the term ἐκκλησία by the Apostles is much easier to understand if it was founded on an impressive saying of our Lord. On the other hand, during our Lord's lifetime such language was peculiarly liable to be misunderstood by the outer world of Jews, and therefore it is not surprising if it formed no part of His ordinary public teaching.

It will be convenient to take first the less important passage, Matt. xviii. 17. Here our Lord is speaking not of the future but the present, instructing

His disciples how to deal with an offending brother. There are three stages of ἔλεγξις, or bringing his fault home to him; first with him alone, next with two or three brethren; and if that fails, thirdly with the ἐκκλησία, the whole brotherhood. The principle holds good in a manner for all time. The actual precept is hardly intelligible if the ἐκκλησία meant is not the Jewish community, apparently the Jewish local community, to which the injured person and the offender both belonged.

We are on quite different ground in the more famous passage, Matt. xvi. 18. At a critical point in the Ministry, far away in the parts of Cæsarea Philippi, our Lord elicits from Peter the confession, "Thou art the Messiah, the Son of the Living God," and pronounces him happy for having been Divinely taught to have the insight which enabled him to make it: "Yea and I say to thee," He proceeds, "that thou art Peter (Πέτρος, *kēphā'*), and on this πέτρα I will build my Ecclesia and the gates of Hades shall not prevail against it."

Here there is no question of a partial or narrowly local Ecclesia. The congregation of God, which held so conspicuous a place in the ancient Scriptures, is assuredly what the disciples could not fail to understand as the foundation of the meaning of a sentence which was indeed for the present mysterious. If we may venture for a moment to substitute the name Israel, and read the words as 'on this rock I will build my Israel,' we gain an impression which supplies at least an approximation to the probable sense. The Ecclesia of the ancient Israel was the Ecclesia of God ; and now, having been confessed to be God's Messiah, nay His Son, He could to such hearers without risk of grave misunderstanding claim that Ecclesia as His own.

What He declared that He would build was in one sense old, in another new. It had a true continuity with the Ecclesia of the Old Covenant; the building of it would be a *re*building[1]. Christ's work in relation to it would be a completion of it, a bestowal on it of power to fulfil its as yet unfulfilled Divine purposes.

But it might also be called a new Ecclesia, as being founded on a new principle or covenant, and in this sense might specially be called the Ecclesia of Messiah, Messiah actually manifested ; and under such a point of view building rather than rebuilding would be the natural verb to use. It is hardly necessary to remind you how these two contrasted aspects of the Gospel, as at once bringing in the new, and fulfilling and restoring the old, are inseparably intertwined in our Lord's teaching.

Hence we shall go greatly astray if we interpret

---

[1] Cf. Acts xv. 16, where James quotes Amos ix. 11, "In that day will I raise up the tabernacle of David that is fallen, and close up the breaches thereof; and I will raise up his ruins, and I *will build* it as in the days of old."

our Lord's use of the term *Ecclesia* in this cardinal passage exclusively by reference to the Ecclesia known to us in Christian history. Speaking with reference to the future, He not only speaks (as the phrase is) "in terms of" the past, but emphatically marks the future as an outgrowth of the past. Here however a question presents itself which we cannot help asking,— asking in all reverence. How came our Lord to make choice of this particular word, or a word belonging to this particular group? Common as are the two Hebrew words which we have examined, *'ēdhāh* and *qāhāl*, they do not occur in any of the important passages which describe or imply the distinctive position of Israel as a peculiar people. Their use is mainly confined to historical parts of the historical book. They have no place in the greater prophecies having what we call a Messianic import. From all parts of the book of Isaiah they are both entirely absent. 'People,' *'ăm*, λαός, is the term which first occurs to us as most often applied to Israel in this as well as in other connexions, and which has also, under limitations, considerable Apostolic sanction as applied to the Christian Ecclesia. But on reflexion we must see, I think, that 'people' was a term which, thus applied, belonged in strictness only to that past period of the world's history in which the society of men specially consecrated to God was likewise a nation, one of many nations, and in the main a race, one of many races. It would have been a true word, but, as used on this occasion, liable to be misunderstood. This impression is confirmed by examination of the passages of the New Testament in which λαός (people) is applied to the Christian Ecclesia. It will be found that they almost always include a direct appropriation of Old Testament language[1].

If the term 'people' was not to be employed, *qāhāl* (ἐκκλησία) was, as far as we can see, the fittest term to take its place. Although, as we saw just now, the use of the two words which we translate 'congregation' and 'assembly' in the Old Testament, is almost wholly historical, not ideal or doctrinal, there is one passage (Ps. lxxiv. 2) in which one of them wears practically another character. It is not a conspicuous passage as it stands in the Psalter; but the manner in which St Paul adopts and adapts its language in his parting address to the Ephesian elders at Miletus (Acts xx. 28) amply justifies the supposition that it helped directly or indirectly to facilitate the use of ἐκκλησία to denote God's people

---

[1] Rom. ix. 25; 2 Cor. vi. 16; Tit. ii. 14; 1 Pet. ii. 9, 10; Heb. viii. 10; Ap. xviii. 4; xxi. 3.

In Heb. iv. 9; xiii. 12 the term includes the ancient people, and is in fact suggested by the purpose of the Epistle as being addressed exclusively to Christians who were also Jews.

In Acts xv. 14 ὁ θεὸς ἐπεσκέψατο λαβεῖν ἐξ ἐθνῶν λαὸν τῷ ὀνόματι αὐτοῦ (Revised Version paraphrastically " God did visit the Gentiles, to take out of them a people for his name "), the paradox of a people of God out of the *Gentiles* explains and justifies itself.

Nor lastly is it a real exception when the Lord tells St Paul in a dream at Corinth that He has " λαὸς πολύς in this city" (Acts xviii. 10).

of the future. "Remember thy congregation which
thou didst purchase of old, didst redeem to be the
tribe of thine inheritance."

The original here is *'ēdhāh*, and the LXX. rendering for it συναγωγή. St Paul substitutes ἐκκλησία
as he also substitutes περιεποιήσατο ('purchased') for
the too colourless ἐκτήσω ('acquired') of the LXX.,
while he further gives the force of the other verb
'redeem' by what he says of the blood through which
the purchase was made. The points that concern us
are these. Not 'people' but 'congregation' is the
word employed by the Psalmist in his appeal to God
on behalf of the suffering Israel of the present, with
reference to what He had wrought for Israel in the
time of old, when He had purchased them out of
Egypt, ransomed them out of Egyptian bondage, to
be a peculiar possession to Himself; these images
of 'purchase' and 'ransom' as applied to the Divine
operation of the Exodus being taken primarily from
the Song of Moses (Exod. xv. 13, 16); and then fresh
significance is given to the Psalmist's language by the
way in which St Paul appropriates it to describe how
God had purchased to Himself a new congregation
(now called ἐκκλησία) by the ransom of His Son's
lifeblood. This seventy-fourth Psalm is now generally
believed to be a very late one; it is not unlikely that
in speaking of God's congregation rather than God's
people, the Psalmist was following a current usage
of his own time. If so, there would be an additional

antecedent leading up to the language which we read in St Matthew. But to say the least, the Psalm shews that such language was not absolutely new[1].

But the fitness of this language by no means depends only on the Psalm or on what the Psalm may imply. These words denoting 'congregation' or 'assembly' had belonged to the children of Israel through their whole history from the day when they became a people. In the written records of the Old Testament they first start forth in this sense in connexion with the institution of the Passover (Ex. xii.): they continue on during the wanderings in the wilderness, in the time of the Judges, under the Kings, and after the Captivity when the kingdom remained unrestored. Moreover they suggested no mere agglomeration of men, but rather a unity carried out in the joint action of many members, each having his own responsibilities, the action of each and all being regulated by a supreme law or order. To Greek ears these words would doubtless be much less significant: but what they suggested would be substantially true as far as it went, and it was not on Greek soil that the earliest Christian Ecclesia was to arise.

This primary sense of ἐκκλησία as a congregation

---

[1] The four passages of the Talmud quoted by Schürer [Eng. Tr. II. ii. p. 59] to shew that *qāhāl* came to have a high ideal character do not at all bear him out.

or assembly of men is not altered by the verb "build" (οἰκοδομήσω) associated with it. It is somewhat difficult for us to feel the exact force of the combination of words, familiar as we are with the idea of building as applied to the material edifice which we call a church, and natural as it is for us to transfer associations unconsciously from the one sense to the other. To speak of men as being built is in accordance with Old Testament usage. Thus Jer. xxiv. 6; I will build them, and not pull them down; and I will plant them, and not pluck them up (cf. xlii. 10); xxxiii. 7, I will cause the captivity of Judah and the captivity of Israel to return, and will build them, as at the first; and elsewhere. But no doubt the singular μου τὴν ἐκκλησίαν is meant to imply more distinctly the building up of the whole body in unity.

What our Lord speaks of however is not simply building, but building "upon this rock." It is impossible now to do more than say in the fewest words that I believe the most obvious interpretation of this famous phrase is the true one. St Peter himself, yet not exclusively St Peter but the other disciples of whom he was then the spokesman and interpreter, and should hereafter be the leader, was the rock which Christ had here in view. It was no question here of an authority given to St Peter; some other image than that of the ground under a foundation must have been chosen if that had been meant. Still less was it a question of an authority which should be transmitted by St Peter to others. The whole was a matter of personal or individual qualifications and personal or individual work. The outburst of keenly perceptive faith had now at last shown St Peter, carrying with him the rest, to have the prime qualification for the task which his Lord contemplated for him.

That task was fulfilled, fulfilled at once and for ever so far as its first and decisive stage was concerned, in the time described in the earliest chapters of the Acts. The combination of intimate personal acquaintance with the Lord, first during His Ministry and then after His Resurrection, with such a faith as was revealed that day in the region of Cæsarea Philippi, a faith which could penetrate into the heavenly truth concerning the Lord that lay beneath the surface of His words and works, these were the qualifications for becoming the foundations of the future Ecclesia. In virtue of this personal faith vivifying their discipleship, the Apostles became themselves the first little Ecclesia, constituting a living rock upon which a far larger and ever enlarging Ecclesia should very shortly be built slowly up, living stone by living stone, as each new faithful convert was added to the society.

But the task thus assigned to St Peter and the rest was not for that generation only. To all future generations and ages the Ecclesia would remain built upon them, upon St Peter and his fellow disciples, partly as a society continuous with the Society which was built directly upon them in, their lifetime, partly as deriving from their faith and experience, as embodied in the New Testament, its whole knowledge of the facts and primary teachings of the Gospel.

The Ecclesia (without the name) in the Gospels.

We must not linger now over the other details of our Lord's words to St Peter; though the time we have already spent on those points in them which most directly concern our subject is hardly out of proportion to their importance in illustration of it. But we have not yet done with the Gospels. Though they contain the word ἐκκλησία but twice, and refer directly to the Christian Ecclesia but once, in other forms they tell much that bears on our subject, far more than it is possible to gather up within our limits. This is one of the cases in which it is dangerous to measure teaching about things by the range of the names applied to things. Much had been done towards the making of the elements of the Ecclesia before its name could with advantage be pronounced otherwise than under such special circumstances as we have just been considering.

One large department of our Lord's teaching, sometimes spoken of as if it directly belonged to our subject, may, I believe, be safely laid aside. In the verse following that which we have been considering, our Lord says to St Peter "I will give thee the keys of the Kingdom of Heaven." Without going into details of interpretation, we can at once see that the relation between the two verses implies some important relation between the Ecclesia and the Kingdom of Heaven: but the question is, what relation? The simplest inference from the language used would be that the office committed to St Peter and the rest with respect to the Ecclesia, would enable him and them to fulfil the office here described as committed to him, with respect to the Kingdom of Heaven. But the question is whether this is a sufficient account of the matter. Since Augustine's time the Kingdom of Heaven or Kingdom of God, of which we read so often in the Gospels, has been simply identified with the Christian Ecclesia. This is a not unnatural deduction from some of our Lord's sayings on this subject taken by themselves; but it cannot, I think, hold its ground when the whole range of His teaching about it is comprehensively examined. We may speak of the Ecclesia as the visible representative of the Kingdom of God, or as the primary instrument of its sway, or under other analogous forms of language. But we are not justified in identifying the one with the other, so as to be able to apply directly to the Ecclesia whatever is said in the Gospels about the Kingdom of Heaven or of God.

On the other hand, wherever we find disciples and

discipleship in the Gospels, there we are dealing with what was a direct preparation for the founding of the Ecclesia. We all know how much more this word 'disciples' sometimes means in the Gospels than admiring and affectionate hearers, though that forms a part of it; how a closer personal relation is further involved in it, for discipleship takes various forms and passes through various stages. Throughout there is devotion to the Lord, found at last to be no mere superior Rabbi, but a true Lord of the spirit; and along with and arising out of this devotion there is a growing sense of brotherhood between disciples.

Chief among the disciples are those Twelve who from certain points of view are called Apostles, but very rarely in the Gospels; sometimes ' The Twelve ', more often simply ' The Disciples '. We do the Evangelists wrong if we treat this use of terms as fortuitous or trivial. It is in truth most exact and most instructive. Not only was discipleship the foundation of apostle-ship, but the Twelve who were Apostles were precisely the men who were most completely disciples. Here we are brought back to the meaning of the building of Christ's Ecclesia upon St Peter and his fellows. The discipleship which accompanied our Lord's Ministry contained, though in an immature form, precisely the conditions by which the Ecclesia sub-sisted afterwards, faith and devotion to the Lord, felt and exercised in union, and consequent brotherly love. It was the strength, so to speak, of St Peter's

discipleship which enabled him, leading the other
eleven disciples and in conjunction with them, to be
a foundation on which fresh growths of the Ecclesia
could be built.

This point needs a little further examination, the
exact relation of the Apostles to the Ecclesia, according to the books of the New Testament, being
a fundamental part of our subject.

LECTURE II.

THE APOSTLES IN RELATION TO THE ECCLESIA.

The term 'Apostle' in the Gospels.

I SAID towards the close of my last lecture that the term 'Apostles' as applied to the Twelve was rare in the Gospels. Let us see what the passages are. The first is a very pregnant one, though simple enough in form, Mark iii. 13–16. Our Lord goes up into the mountain, and "calls to Him whom He Himself would, and they departed unto Him. And He made twelve, whom He also named Apostles, [such is assuredly the true reading, though the common texts create an artificial smoothness by omitting the last clause] that they should be with Him, and that He should send ($\dot{a}\pi o\sigma\tau\dot{\epsilon}\lambda\lambda\eta$) them to preach and to have authority to cast out the demons; and He made the Twelve...Peter (giving this name to Simon) and James etc." Here by what seems to be a double process of selection (though the

word selection is not used), proceeding wholly from
Himself, our Lord sets aside twelve for two great
purposes, kept apart in the Greek by the double ἵνα :
the first, personal nearness to Himself "that they
should be with Him": the second, "with a view to
sending them forth", this mission of theirs having
two heads, to preach, and to have authority to cast
out the 'demons', these two being precisely the two
modes of action which St Mark has described in
i. 39 as exercised by the Lord Himself in the
synagogues of all Galilee, just as in the previous
verses i. 14–34 he had described a succession of acts
which came under these heads, the second head
evidently including the healing of the sick. Lastly
we learn that our Lord Himself, apparently on this
occasion, called these twelve chosen men 'Apostles'
or 'envoys'.

Whether they were or were not sent forth immediately after this their selection, St Mark does
not expressly tell us. But it is morally certain that
he intended to represent the actual mission as *not*
immediate. Such is the natural force of ἵνα ἀπο-
στέλλῃ "with a view to sending them forth", and
moreover more than one hundred verses further
on (vi. 7) we read how when our Lord was going
round the villages teaching, He called to Himself the Twelve, "and *began* to send them forth by
two and two"; and so, after a brief account of His
charge to them we read (vi. 12 f.) "and they went

out and preached that men should repent, and they cast out many demons, and anointed with oil many that were sick and healed them":—again the two heads of what they were to do when sent forth. Then comes the story of Herod and John the Baptist ; and then (vi. 30) "and the Apostles are gathered together (συνάγονται) unto Jesus, and they told Him all things whatsoever they had *done* and whatsoever they had *taught*" (again the two heads emphatically distinguished). Henceforward the word ἀπόστολος disappears from St Mark's Gospel; so that he evidently used it only in the strictest sense, with reference to this one typical mission to preach and to heal, at the beginning of it and at the end of it. When he wishes afterwards[1] to mark them out sharply from the other disciples, he calls them "the Twelve."

Next, St Luke's Gospel is interesting both by its resemblances and by its differences. First comes a passage (vi. 12 ff.) which includes in itself both likeness and unlikeness to St Mark. "It came to pass in these days that He went out unto the mountain to pray, and He continued all night in His prayer to God. And when it was day, He called His disciples, and choosing from them twelve, whom He also named Apostles, Simon..., and going down with them, He stood on a level place." Here

---

[1] See St Mark ix. 35 ; x. 32 ; xi. 11 ; xiv. 17: besides the Judas passages (xiv. 10, 20, 43).

the selection by our Lord is mentioned, and the
name 'Apostles' which He gave: but nothing is
said of either purpose or work. The selection is
associated with the Sermon on the Mount. We do
hear however (vi. 17 f.) of the great crowd who
were present "to hear Him" (the correlative of
preaching) "and to be healed of their diseases",
"unclean spirits" being mentioned in the next
sentence. Then, after a considerable interval, we
read (ix. 1) how He called together the Twelve (the
addition "Apostles" has high authority but is
probably only an Alexandrine reading), and gave
them power and authority over all demons and to
cure diseases, and sent them forth (ἀπέστειλεν) to
preach the kingdom of God and to heal. After a
charge of three verses only, we read (ix. 6) "And they
going forth went throughout the villages, *preaching*
good tidings and *healing* everywhere". (Thus the two
heads are twice repeated). Then Herod is spoken
of for three verses, and in *v.* 10 (just as in Mark vi.
30) we have the Twelve on their *return* described
as Apostles, "And the Apostles when they had
returned recounted to Him what they had done."
If we pursue the narrative a little further, we shall
hardly think this limitation of usage accidental. Two
verses later (ix. 12) it is the Twelve who are said to
come to our Lord and bid Him dismiss the multitude.
In *v.* 14 they are called "His disciples", in *vv.* 16, 18
"the disciples", and so on.

In this Gospel however the term is not throughout confined to this limited usage. Three times afterwards[1] it speaks of "the Apostles", without any perceptible reference to that mission, while it also speaks of 'the Twelve' once[2] and of 'the Eleven' twice[3]. The explanation, I suppose, is that St Luke, having probably in his mind the writing of the Acts, which is (see Acts i. 1 f.) a kind of second part to the Gospel, in these three places used by anticipation the title which, as we shall see presently, acquired a fresh currency after the Ascension: in each of the three cases the accompanying language bears no trace of coming from a common source with anything in the other Gospels; so that the wording is probably entirely St Luke's own. The anticipatory use thus supposed has no doubt an instructiveness of its own. It serves to remind us how all that period, in which the Twelve seemed to be only gathering in *personal* gains to heart and mind by their discipleship, was in truth the indispensable condition and, as it were, education for their future action upon others.

St Matthew on the other hand gives even less prominence to the title 'Apostles' than St Mark. He tells us (x. 1) that our Lord "calling His twelve disciples unto Him gave them authority over unclean

---

[1] See St Luke xvii. 5; xxii. 14 (the right reading); xxiv. 10.

[2] St Luke xviii. 31, besides the reference to Judas, xxii. 47.

[3] St Luke xxiv. 9 (just before τοὺς ἀποστόλους), 33.

spirits so as to cast them out and to heal every disease and every sickness." " Now the names of the twelve Apostles," he adds, " are these…." In the other two Gospels we have had two separate incidents, the selection on the mountain, and the subsequent mission among the villages. Here in St Matthew the first incident is dropped altogether, so that in the first words of chap. x. " His twelve disciples " are spoken of as an already known or already existing body to whom powers are now given, and the list of names is prefixed to the account of their mission. We are not told that our Lord called them 'Apostles' nor is any other indication given that the term had a special meaning: nay, the word in this context might with at least as great propriety be translated 'envoys' as 'Apostles'. The nature of their mission is not expressly described, though our Lord's own previous action is spoken of (ix. 35) as "teaching in their synagogues and preaching the Gospel of the kingdom and curing every disease and every sickness." But St Matthew places here the well-known charge, introducing it with the words " These twelve Jesus sent (ἀπέστειλεν) charging them saying," etc., and the charge itself almost at once puts forward the same heads of mission which we have found in the other Gospels. Thenceforward St Matthew never uses the term 'Apostle'. When he needs a precise designation, it is usually[1], " His

---

twelve disciples" or "the Twelve[1]", and once (xxviii. 16) "the eleven disciples".

St John's usage, as is well-known, is more remarkable still. He never calls the Twelve "Apostles", unless it be by indirect allusion (xiii. 16) "A servant is not greater than his lord; neither an envoy (one sent) greater than he that sent him." Of the Twelve he speaks in vi. 67, 70 "Jesus said therefore to the Twelve 'Will ye also go?'" "Did not I choose you the Twelve, and one of you is a διάβολος?"; besides his use of the term to describe Judas (vi. 71) and Thomas (xx. 24).

Taking these facts together respecting the usage of the Gospels, we are led, I think, to the conclusion that in its original sense the term Apostle was not intended to describe the habitual relation of the Twelve to our Lord during the days of His ministry, but strictly speaking only that mission among the villages, of which the beginning and the end are recorded for us; just as in the Acts, Paul and Barnabas are called Apostles (i.e. of the Church of Antioch) with reference to that special mission which we call St Paul's First Missionary Journey, and to that only. At the same time this limited apostleship was not heterogeneous from the apostleship of later days spoken of in the Acts, but a prelude to it, a preparation for it, and as

[1] See St Matt. xx. 17 *v. l.*; xxvi. 20 *v. l.* besides the Judas passages, xxvi. 14, 47.

it were a type of it. Such sayings as that difficult one (Matt. xix. 28 ‖ Luke xxii. 30) about sitting on twelve thrones, judging the twelve tribes of Israel, are indications that a distinctive function was reserved for the Twelve throughout, over and above their function as the chiefest disciples. It remains true that the habitual, always appropriate, designations of the Twelve during our Lord's ministry were simply "the disciples" or "the twelve" or "the twelve disciples".

And this use of names points to corresponding facts. Discipleship, not apostleship, was the primary active function, so to speak, of the Twelve till the Ascension, and, as we shall see, it remained always their fundamental function. The purpose of their being with Him (with the Lord) stands first in that memorable sentence of St Mark, and is sharply distinguished from the Lord's second purpose in forming them into a body, viz. the sending them forth to preach and to work acts of deliverance. But the distinction does not rest on those words alone. A far larger proportion of the Gospels is taken up with records of facts belonging to the discipleship than with records of facts belonging to the apostleship, so far as it is possible to distinguish them.

The Last Supper.

When the Ministry is over, and the end is beginning, the importance of the special discipleship of the

Twelve in relation to the future Ecclesia soon comes
to light. The Last Supper is the most solemn and
characteristic gathering together of the Twelve with
the Lord at their head. There in the upper room
they are completely "*with Him*," and completely
separated from all others. The words and acts at
this supper, which constitute the institution of the
Holy Communion, were addressed to the Twelve, and
no others are spoken of as recipients of the command.
Whatever directions for the future are present here
are contained within the simple imperatives addressed
to the Twelve, "take," "eat," "drink," and (if we add
St Paul and the interpolation in St Luke's text
derived from him) "do this." Of whom then in after
times were the Twelve the representatives that evening?
If they represented an apostolic order within the
Ecclesia then the Holy Communion must have been
intended only for members of that order, and the rest
of the Ecclesia had no part in it. But if, as the men
of the Apostolic age and subsequent ages believed
without hesitation, the Holy Communion was meant
for the Ecclesia at large, then the Twelve sat that
evening as representatives of the Ecclesia at large :
they were disciples more than they were Apostles.

That central event of the Last Supper, as we all
know, is not mentioned by St John : but there is a
close connexion between its meaning and much of
the contents of those five chapters of his Gospel, from
the thirteenth to the seventeenth, which begin with the

washing of St Peter's feet, and end with the Lord's own
last prayer before His departure from the city for the
garden. Though the word *ecclesia* does not occur
in these chapters, any more than in the rest of the
Gospel, the inward characteristics of the Christian
Ecclesia according to Christ's intention are virtually
expounded in not a few of their verses. The seclusion
of the Twelve, soon becoming the Eleven, with their
Lord away from all other men, makes itself felt
throughout: but it is equally clear that the little band
of chosen ones, with whom those marvellous discourses
were held, was destined to become no mere partial
order of men but a people of God, an Ecclesia like the
ideal Israel. The feet-washing in act, and the new
commandment in words, lay down the primary law
for the mutual action of the members of the Ecclesia,
humility and love; the similitude of the vine and the
branches lays down their common relation to their
Divine Head. The promise of the other Paraclete,
the Spirit of the Truth, and the exposition of His
working, are a new and pregnant revelation of life and
light for the Ecclesia. In the last prayer the goal of
unity is set forth in a sentence (xvii. 20) which expressly
recognises the growth of the future Ecclesia from that
little band: "Neither for these only do I pray, but
for them also that believe on me through their word;
that they may all be one; even as Thou, Father, art in
me, and I in Thee, that they also may be in us; that
the world may believe that Thou didst send me."

These last words bring out the purpose of the Ecclesia in God's counsels : it is to draw the rest of mankind to its own faith and love; to carry on a work of salvation, in the power of the salvation wrought by its Head : "as Thou didst send me into the world, I also sent them into the world." The whole Ecclesia shares alike in that transmitted Mission.

The utterances after the Resurrection.

Before we pass from the Gospels we must look for a moment at one or two famous passages belonging to the days after the Resurrection, especially to the last five verses of St Matthew, and to our Lord's appearance among the disciples on the evening of the first day of the week (John xx. 19–23), when He breathed on them and said "Receive ye the Holy Spirit...." To discuss the contents of these passages would carry us into matters which it is happily not necessary to our purpose to examine in detail. But it is needful to point out the bearing of the results at which we have hitherto arrived, on the question as to the recipients of these two famous sets of words. Much stress is often laid on the supposed evidence afforded by the words of the evangelists that they were addressed exclusively to the Apostles. Dr Westcott has shown how, when we look below the surface, indications are not wanting that others were not improbably likewise present, at all events on the occasion recorded by St John, when his narrative is compared with that of St Luke (xxiv. 33 ff.).

But in such a matter the mere fact that doubt is possible is a striking one. It is in truth difficult to separate these cases from the frequent omission of the evangelists to distinguish the Twelve from other disciples; a manner of language which, as we have seen, explains itself at once when we recognise how large a part discipleship played in the function of the Twelve.

Granting that it was probably to the Eleven that our Lord directly and principally spoke on both these occasions (and even to them alone when He spoke the words at the end of St Matthew's Gospel), yet it still has to be considered in what capacity they were addressed by Him. If at the Last Supper, and during the discourses which followed, when the Twelve or Eleven were most completely secluded from all other disciples as well as from the unbelieving Jews, they represented the whole Ecclesia of the future, it is but natural to suppose that it was likewise as representatives of the whole Ecclesia of the future, whether associated with other disciples or not, that they had given to them those two assurances and charges of our Lord, about the receiving of the Holy Spirit and the remitting or retaining of sins (howsoever we understand these words), and about His universal authority in heaven and on earth, on the strength of which He bids them bring all the nations into discipleship, and assures them of His own presence with them all the days even to the consummation of the age.

This interpretation is not affected by the special language used in Matt. xxviii. 19, where bringing all the nations into discipleship is coupled with baptizing them into the Threefold Name. In the most literal sense of these words, they apply to the bearers of the message of the Gospel, chief among whom, ideally at least, were the Apostles; though the personal act of baptizing is somewhat markedly disconnected from evangelistic work by St Paul in 1 Cor. i. 14–17. In a word, the action of the Apostles is the most obvious expression, so to speak, of the charge then given. But the work of the Ecclesia in relation to the world is itself a missionary work ; and it is to the Ecclesia itself as the missionary body that Christ's charge is ultimately addressed.

The new Apostolic mission.

On entering the Acts of the Apostles, we come at once to the term 'apostles'. It continues with us all through the book with the rarest exceptions[1]. This

[1] When the excitement caused by the miracle of Pentecost leads to St Peter's first discourse to the people it is said, "And Peter standing *with the Eleven* lifted up his voice and spake forth to them." So when the neglect of the Greek-speaking widows led to the appointment of the seven whom we call deacons, it is "the Twelve" who are said to call to them "the multitude of the disciples" (vi. 2). And once we have the compound term (i. 26), when Matthias is said to have been numbered "with the eleven Apostles".

fact suggests that a change has passed upon the work or office of the Twelve : and such we actually find.

Two points especially require notice. Their original mission, from which apparently proceeded the title 'apostle' given them by our Lord, was strictly confined to Judæa (Matt. x. 5 f.), "Go not into any way of the Gentiles, and enter not into any city of the Samaritans : but go rather to the lost sheep of the house of Israel." And the same charge which opens with these words contains the remarkable and by no means easy sentence (Matt. x. 23), "When they persecute you in this city, flee into the next; for verily I say unto you, Ye shall not have gone through the cities of Israel, till the Son of man be come." The limitation of the original apostolic mission here indicated is maintained strictly in the Gospels throughout the Ministry. Whatever tokens or express declarations of the destination of the Gospel for all nations may be recorded by the Evangelists in this part of their books, in no case, I believe, is any reference there made to the agency of the Apostles in extending the sphere of the message of salvation. No doubt it is sometimes said that the prediction of the Apostles being brought before rulers and kings (ἡγεμόνες and βασιλεῖς), which St Matthew places in that same first charge to the Apostles which we have just been looking at (x. 18), and St Mark and St Luke in the discourse of judgement pronounced on the Mount of Olives in the last week (Mark xiii. 9 ;

Luke xxi. 12), it is said, I say, that this prediction must refer to the heathen magistrates and potentates who withstood the Gospel in various parts of the Roman Empire. The words are however quite as naturally applicable to heathen rulers who, no less than the Jewish authorities, would be found hostile in Judæa itself. The allusion is, I strongly suspect, to the enemies of Jehovah and His Anointed, called in Ps. ii. 2 "the kings of the earth and the rulers" (LXX. ἄρχοντες), a description which the Apostles recognise as fulfilled in Herod and Pontius Pilate as gathered together against our Lord Himself (Acts iv. 27), thus making a hostile combination of Gentiles with Jews.

The extension of the range of the apostolic mission takes place between the Resurrection and the Ascension. Not to dwell again on the last charge at the end of St Matthew's Gospel, nor to refer by more than a word to the version of it preserved in a record of such uncertain authority as the Appendix to St Mark's Gospel, we read in Luke xxiv. 45 ff. how our Lord opened their mind to understand the Scriptures, and said to them that "thus it is written," not only "that the Christ should suffer and rise again on the third day," but also "that repentance unto remission of sins should be preached (or proclaimed) in His Name unto all the nations, beginning with Jerusalem." "Ye are witnesses," he adds, "of these things."

This language is strikingly guarded. The going

forth of the message of salvation is set forth as involved in the vision of the future which the prophets were permitted to see; but it is set forth wholly impersonally: nothing connects the Apostles themselves with it but the single saying "Ye are witnesses of these things"; a saying which perfectly well admits of meaning no more than that the fundamental testimony of "these things" (itself an elastic phrase) was to be given by the Apostles, without further implying that they were to be themselves the bearers of the message founded on that testimony to heathen lands.

Of less ambiguous import are the words which we read in Acts i. 8 as spoken to them by the Lord just before the Ascension, "Ye shall be my witnesses both in Jerusalem and in all Judæa and Samaria and unto the utmost part of the earth." Here the utmost range seems to be given to the testimony which they are to bear in person; and this, the most obvious sense, is confirmed by the previous sentence, "But ye shall receive power by the Holy Spirit coming upon you," such power from above being evidently intended to sustain them in their long and troubled course of bearing witness. Thus universality is a characteristic of the new apostolic mission.

In what manner the Twelve understood themselves afterwards to be charged with this enlarged responsibility, it is difficult to make out. The admission of the Gentiles was assuredly not accepted at once without hesitation as a necessary consequence of the terms of the Lord's commission. But the mere recognition of His having at this solemn time so expressly dwelt on the ultimate world-wide destination of His Gospel, must have been enough to affect deeply the character of their work, even in its first and narrowest sphere at Jerusalem.

The second characteristic of the new apostolic mission is that which has already come before us in connexion with its universality,—its work of bearing witness. This comes out with especial clearness in St Peter's address to the brethren respecting providing a successor to Judas: "Of the men," he says (i. 21 f.), "that companied with us all the time that the Lord Jesus came in and went out unto us, beginning from the baptism of John unto the day that He was received up from us, of these must one become a witness with us of His Resurrection." This is the one essential condition mentioned, to be a witness of the Resurrection. The prayer that follows describes the office itself as "the place of this ministration and mission" (τῆς διακονίας ταύτης καὶ ἀποστολῆς) just as St Peter had previously (*v.* 17) called it "the lot of this ministration." But this does not alter the statement as to the indispensable qualification. Nor does this passage stand alone. Everyone must remember the persistency with which this apostolic witness-bearing to the crowning events of Gospel history is reiterated in the Acts, and especially in the early speeches in the Acts (ii. 32, iii. 15, iv. 33, v. 32, x. 39–41, xiii. 31).

This mark of apostleship is evidently founded on direct personal discipleship; and as evidently it is incommunicable. Its whole meaning rested on immediate and unique experience; as St John says, "that which we have heard, that which we have seen with our eyes, that which we beheld, and our hands handled" (1 John i. 1). Without a true perceptive faith, such a faith as shewed itself in St Peter, all this acquaintance through the bodily senses was in vain. But the truest faith of one who was a disciple only in the second degree, however precious in itself, could never qualify him for bearing the apostolic character.

Apart from this unique function of being witnesses of the Resurrection, it is difficult to find in the New Testament any clear definition of the Apostolic office from the records of the time between the Resurrection and the Ascension. In the second verse of the Acts we read of our Lord giving them command (ἐντειλάμενος) on the day of His Ascension: but what were the contents of that commandment we know not, unless it was the charge to continue at Jerusalem awaiting the promise of the Father, the Pentecostal gift (i. 4, 5; Luke xxiv. 49). So again in *v.* 3 we hear of His "appearing to them and saying to them the things concerning the kingdom of God": but more than this we do not learn. What Scripture says, and what it

leaves unsaid, together suggest that the new stage of
Apostleship was inaugurated by no new act of
appointment analogous to the original designation of
the Twelve on the mountain, these commands and
teachings that we hear of being rather like the
subsequent charge to the Apostles on their going
forth among the villages. On this view it was the
Crucifixion (interpreted as always by the Resurrection)
which constituted the real inauguration of the renewed apostleship. We saw the other day how the
work assigned to the Twelve, when first sent forth
among the villages, was a repetition, so to speak,
of the work which our Lord Himself was then
pursuing, consisting of two heads, preaching and
casting out demons, including the healing of sickness;
or in other words, proclaiming the kingdom of God
by word, and manifesting and illustrating it by
significant act. The work that lay before them
when His Ministry on earth was ended was not in its
essence different from before : they had still to make
known the kingdom of God by words and by deeds;
and this is the sole conception of their work put
before us in the Acts. But there were two great
changes. First, He Himself would no longer be
visibly in their midst, so that the responsibility of
guidance descended upon them, subject only to the
indications of His Will, and enlightened by His Spirit.
Moreover, this responsibility was not for a limited
mission of short duration, but by its very nature was

continuous and permanent. Second, He Himself, in His Death and His Resurrection, was now become a primary subject of their teaching and action : in the light of Him the kingdom of God put on a new meaning, and He was Himself the living representative of it.

LECTURE III.

EARLY STAGES IN THE GROWTH OF THE ECCLESIA.

WE now enter on the narrative of the time which followed the Ascension, limiting ourselves as far as possible to those parts of St Luke's record which illustrate the characteristics of the new Ecclesia and the stages of its growth ; but not neglecting either pieces of evidence relating to the Ecclesia under other names and descriptions, or the history of the use of the name *ecclesia* itself.

On the return from the Mount of Olives the eleven remaining Apostles go up into the upper chamber where they were staying (i. 13), and thus renew, as it were, their coherence as a definite body.

A somewhat larger body is next mentioned as "attending steadfastly with one accord upon 'the prayer'," certain women, and the Lord's mother and brethren, being associated with the Apostles.

This peculiar phrase taken in conjunction with "the prayers" (ii. 42) and "the prayer" (vi. 4) suggests that a definite custom of common prayer is intended, a bond of Christian fellowship.

Next in *v.* 15 we read of a larger assembly, probably the whole body of 'brethren,' as they are emphatically called, about 120 in number. " In the midst of the brethren," St Luke says, St Peter rose up and declared the need of filling up the place left vacant by Judas.

The next chapter relates the appearance of the fiery tongues on the day of Pentecost, St Peter's discourse, and the results of it. The hearers, or some of them, are pricked to the heart and ask Peter and the other Apostles, whom they recognise as brother Israelites (ἄνδρες ἀδελφοί), " What shall we do ?" The answer is " Repent ye, and let each one of you be baptised in the name of Jesus Christ unto remission of your sins, and ye shall receive the gift of the Holy Spirit: for to you is the promise and to your children and to all that are afar off, as many as the Lord our God shall call unto Him." The other recorded words of his exhortation are significant, " Save yourselves from this crooked generation." This phrase 'crooked generation' comes, you may remember, from what is said of the rebellious Israelites in the wilderness in Deut. xxxii. 5. There is not a word against the ancient Ecclesia or people. The crooked generation of the unbelieving present, which perverts and misinterprets

the ancient covenant, is the evil sphere to be
abandoned.

These men accept his discourse and are baptised. That is the definite act which signifies at
once their faith in Jesus as Messiah, and thereby
their joining of themselves to the society of His
disciples; and on the other hand the acceptance of
them by the Ecclesia. "And there were added on
that day about three thousand souls."

Then comes the description of the characteristic
acts and practices by which these new members lived
the life of members of the new brotherhood. "They
continued attending steadfastly upon (προσκαρτεροῦν-
τες) the teaching of the Apostles and upon the communion, upon the breaking of the bread and upon the
prayers." In the centre we see the apostolic body, a
bond of unity to the rest. Their public teaching,
replacing the public teaching of the scribes, carries
on the instruction of converts who have yet much to
learn, and attendance upon it is at the same time
a mark of fellowship. Next comes what is called
' the communion ', conduct expressive of and resulting
from the strong sense of fellowship with the other
members of the brotherhood, probably public acts by
which the rich bore some of the burdens of the poor.
Thirdly we have ' the breaking of the bread,' what
we call the Holy Communion, named here from the
expressive act by which the unity of the many as
partakers of the one Divine sustenance is signified.

Lastly we have 'the prayers', apparently Christian prayers in common, which took the place of the prayers of the synagogues.

In the next group of verses we hear not merely of these new disciples, but of the whole body of which they had now become members. "All that believed together" says St Luke (this is his peculiar but pregnant description of membership), "all that believed together had all things common; and they sold their possessions and goods, and parted them to all, according as any man had need." This general statement is qualified and explained later. Evidently there was no law of the society imposing such sale : but the principle of holding all in trust for the benefit of the rest of the community was its principle of possession. "And day by day", the narrative proceeds, "attending steadfastly with one accord in the temple, and breaking bread at home, they partook of their food in exultation ($\dot{a}\gamma a\lambda\lambda\iota\dot{a}\sigma\epsilon\iota$) and singleness of heart, praising God and having favour with all the people. And the Lord added to their company day by day them that were saved" (or Revised Version, "were being saved": neither rendering satisfactory). Such is St Luke's account of the inward spirit and outward demeanour of the new Ecclesia, not yet in any antagonism to the old Ecclesia but the most living portion of it, and manifestly laying claim by attendance in the temple to be a society of loyal sons of Israel.

Thus far St Luke has been picturing to us the Christian Ecclesia of Jerusalem antecedent to all persecution, moved simply by its own inherent principles. A fresh impulse towards consolidation comes from the onslaught of the Jewish authorities, due to the healing of the lame man at the Beautiful Gate of the Temple, an event which had at once caused an increase in the number of Christian believers so that they reached five thousand (iv. 4). Peter and John, threatened by the Council, return "to their own company" (τοὺς ἰδίους), almost certainly, I think, the apostolic company ; and together they pour forth a prayer in which they recognise that now they too are having to encounter the same opposition which by God's own providence had fallen upon His holy servant Jesus whom He anointed ; and they ask to be enabled to speak His word with all boldness while He stretches forth His hand for healing, and for signs and wonders to come to pass through the name of His holy servant Jesus : thus attesting once more in the most solemn way the two original heads of the active functions assigned to them.

In St Luke's narrative this incident is followed by an emphatic statement that the multitude (πλῆθος) of them that believed had but one heart and soul, and a renewal in more precise terms of the former statement about their having all things common. " And with great power," he proceeds (iv. 33), " did the

Apostles of the Lord Jesus deliver their testimony of His Resurrection, and great joy was upon them all ". The absence of want among them (οὐδὲ γὰρ ἐνδεής τις ἦν) is given as a reason for this joy, the needs of the poor being provided for by the sale of lands or houses. In the former passage of similar import (ii. 44 f.), we read only of a distribution of the purchase money by the members of the community at large, or possibly by the vendors themselves. Here on the other hand we read that the purchase money was brought and laid at the Apostles' feet for distribution, and further that Joseph, whom the Apostles called Barnabas for his power of exhortation, sold a field and laid the price at the Apostles' feet. This is the first indication of the exercise of powers of administration by the Apostles, and, so far as appears, it was not the result of an authority claimed by them but of a voluntary entrusting of the responsibility to the Apostles by the rest. It was probably now felt that the functions and powers Divinely conferred upon them for preaching and healing as witnesses of the Resurrection, marked them out likewise as the fit persons to deal with the responsibilities of administration in carrying out the mutual bearing of burdens. The manner in which Barnabas's name is introduced is remarkable, as also the express mention of his laying the value of his field at the Apostles' feet. It does not seem unlikely that this important step on the part of the Ecclesia was taken at Barnabas's

suggestion; just as with no less boldness and fore-
thought he brought St Paul into close relations with
the Twelve at Jerusalem (ix. 27), and encouraged the
newly founded Ecclesia at Antioch at a sufficiently
critical time (xi. 22–24).

The event which comes next, the falsehood and
death of Ananias and Sapphira, is for our purpose
instructive in more ways than one. First, St Peter's
words "While it (the land) remained, did it not remain
thine own? and after it was sold was it not in thine
own power (or right, ἐξουσίᾳ)?" exhibit the real nature
of the community of goods at this time practised in
the Christian community. There was no merging of
all private possessions in a common stock, but a
voluntary and variable contribution on a large scale.
That is to say, the Ecclesia was a society in which
neither the community was lost in the individuals, nor
the individuals in the community. The community
was set high above all, while the service and help to
be rendered to the community remained a matter of
individual conscience and free bounty. Next, the
reality of the bond uniting together the members of
the Christian community was vindicated in the most
impressive way by the Divine judgment which fell on
Ananias and Sapphira by the shock at the discovery
of their deceit. Falsehood or faithlessness towards
the Holy Spirit, as St Peter calls it, was involved in
their faithlessness to the community, affecting as they
did to take part to the full in the lofty life of mutual

help, while their hypocritical reservation made brotherly fellowship an unreality. In consequence of
this occurrence "great fear," we are told, "fell on the
whole Ecclesia, and all that heard these things." Up
to this time, as Bengel points out, St Luke has used
only such descriptive phrases as "they that believed",
"the brethren" etc. Now for the first time he speaks
of the Ecclesia. Whether it was so called at the time,
·it is not easy to tell. No approach to separation from
the great Jewish Ecclesia had as yet taken place. On
the other hand our Lord's saying to St Peter must
have been always present to the minds of the Apostles,
and can hardly have been without influence on their
early teaching. If St Luke used the word here by
anticipation, it was doubtless with a wish to emphasise
·the fact that the death of Ananias and Sapphira
marked an epoch in the early growth of the society,
a time when its distinctness, and the cohesion of its
members, had come to be distinctly recognised without
as well as within.

A short period of prosperity follows (v. 12 ff.). By
the hands of the Apostles many miracles are wrought
among the people. They were all with one accord in
the great arcade called Solomon's Porch, reaching
along the whole east side of the vast Temple precinct.
"Of the rest," says St Luke, meaning apparently those
who elsewhere are distinguished from "the people",
the priests, rulers, elders, scribes, "no one dared to

H. E. 4

cleave to them (*i.e.* however much he may have
secretly become in conviction a Christian), but *the
people* magnified them, and yet more were added to
them, believing the Lord, multitudes of men and
women ". Even the neighbouring towns, we read, contributed their sick and possessed, who came to be
healed. This fresh success leads to a fresh imprison-
ment of the Apostles ; but by Gamaliel's advice they
are dismissed with a scourging and warning. But
they continue day by day in the Temple and in
private houses to proclaim the good tidings.

The appointment of the Seven.

We now come to an incident which concerns us
both as itself a step in the organisation of the Ecclesia, and as a prelude to an event which had decisive
effects on the position of the Ecclesia as a whole, the
martyrdom of Stephen. This incident is the appointment of the Seven, answering to a great extent to
those who were later called deacons. As the disciples
multiplied, complaints were made by the Greek-
speaking Jews settled in Jerusalem that their widows
were neglected in the daily ministration ($\delta\iota\alpha\kappa o\nu\iota\alpha$) for
the relief of the poor, in comparison with the widows
belonging to the Hebrew part of the community.
The Twelve call to them the multitude ($\tau\grave{o}\ \pi\lambda\hat{\eta}\theta o\varsigma$)
of the disciples and say " It is not right (or desirable
$\mathring{a}\rho\epsilon\sigma\tau\acute{o}\nu$) that we, leaving the word of God, should serve
tables ($\delta\iota\alpha\kappa o\nu\epsilon\hat{\iota}\nu\ \tau\rho\alpha\pi\acute{e}\zeta\alpha\iota\varsigma$) : but look ye out, brethren,

men from among yourselves of good report, seven in number, full of the Spirit and of wisdom, whom we will set over this office (or need, χρείας means either): but we will attend diligently upon the prayer and upon the ministration (διακονίᾳ) of the word." The suggestion found favour with all the multitude. They chose out seven, including a proselyte from Antioch, and set them before the Apostles, who prayed and laid their hands on them. It is impossible not to connect this act with the laying of the contributions at the Apostles' feet. As being thus constituted stewards of the bounty of the community they were in a manner responsible for the distribution of the charitable fund. But the task had outgrown their powers, unless it was to be allowed to encroach on their higher Divinely appointed functions. They proposed therefore to entrust this special part of the work to other men, having the prerequisites of devoutness and wisdom, to be chosen by the Ecclesia at large. How much this new office included is not easy to say. All the seven names being Greek, it seems probable that they were Hellenists, as otherwise it would be a strange coincidence that there should be no Hebrew names; and if so, it would also seem likely that they were charged only with the care of relief to Hellenists. We do not hear however of any analogous office for the Hebrew Christians, nor whether any general superintendence of the funds was still retained by the Apostles. Nor again do we

4—2

afterwards hear anything more of these Seven in
relation to their special work. The definite recognition of special claims of Christian Hellenists was the
essential point. Stephen's miracles and preaching
were no part of his office as one of the Seven, though
they may have led to his selection; and Philip in
like manner is known only as doing the work of an
evangelist.

But the appointment was not only a notable
recognition of the Hellenistic element in the Ecclesia
at Jerusalem, a prelude of greater events to come, but
also a sign that the Ecclesia was to be an Ecclesia
indeed, not a mere horde of men ruled absolutely by
the Apostles, but a true body politic, in which different
functions were assigned to different members, and a
share of responsibility rested upon the members at
large, each and all; while every work for the Ecclesia,
high and low, was of the nature of a 'ministration', a
true rendering of a servant's service.

Once more we hear that "the word of God grew,
and the number of disciples in Jerusalem multiplied
exceedingly, and a great multitude of the priests
obeyed the faith." A little while ago it would seem
that they were among those mentioned in v. 13 as not
daring to cleave or join themselves to the Ecclesia.
But now their faith had grown stronger and deeper;
and one after another they obeyed its call, and took
the risks of joining the Christian congregation.

The Ecclesia spreading throughout the Holy Land.

We may pass over the discourse and martyrdom of Stephen. But the verse which follows the recital of his death (viii. 1) deserves our special attention for its language, and the facts which account for its language. "There came in that day a great persecution upon the Ecclesia which was in Jerusalem (τὴν ἐκκλησίαν τὴν ἐν Ἱεροσολύμοις): all were scattered abroad about the regions of Judæa and Samaria save the Apostles ". In the single place where the word *Ecclesia* has before occurred in the Acts (v. 11), there has been no question of more than the one Ecclesia of all Christ's disciples. Here we have that same identical body, differing only by the reception of more numerous members, so described as to give a hint that soon there were to be in a true sense of the word (though not the only true sense) more Ecclesiae than one. The materials for new Ecclesiae were about to be formed in consequence of this temporary scattering of the original Ecclesia ; and moreover this first wide carrying of the Gospel through Judæa and Samaria was not the work of the Apostles : they are specially excepted by St Luke. Parenthetically in viii. 3 we read how Saul ravaged the Ecclesia, entering in house by house : and here the Ecclesia just spoken of, that of Jerusalem, seems to be meant, his prosecution of the persecution elsewhere even to Damascus being probably later. Of the work of one of the scattered

Christians, Philip the evangelist, we hear specially, its
sphere being the representative city of Samaria.
Tidings of his successful preaching and his baptizing
of men and women having reached the Apostles at
Jerusalem ("hearing that Samaria hath received the
word of God" viii. 14), they depute Peter and John to
go down.   They found apparently no reason to doubt
the reality and sincerity of the conversions.   But the
recognition of Samaritans as true members of the
Christian community, hitherto exclusively Jewish, was
so important a step outwards from the first, and now
by long custom established, state of things that they
evidently shrank from giving full and unreserved welcome to the new converts, unless they could obtain
a conspicuous Divine sanction, what is called in this
book receiving the (or a) Holy Spirit.   What is meant
is shown clearly by comparison with x. 44-48 and
xix. 6, 7, *viz.* the outward marvellous signs of the
Spirit, such as manifested themselves on the Day of
Pentecost, speaking with tongues, with or without
prophesying.   "These which received the Holy Spirit
even as we did" (x. 47) is the phrase in which St Peter
describes the Divine sanction which justified recognition for Christian discipleship and membership.   In
this case the baptism of the Samaritan converts had
been followed by no such tokens from heaven, and so
they prayed for them that they might receive the
Holy Spirit, and then laid their hands on them (the
human symbolic act answering to the Heavenly act

prayed for) and they received the Holy Spirit (ἐλάμ-
βανον not ἔλαβον), that is, shewed a succession of
signs of the Spirit. After the interlude of Simon
Magus the Apostles return to Jerusalem, and on the
way they themselves preach the Gospel to many
Samaritan villages.

We need not examine the story of Philip and the
eunuch, or even the conversion of St Paul, his
recovery from blindness, preaching at Damascus,
escape from attempted murder, admission to the
confidence of the Apostles by the instrumentality of
Barnabas, and on a fresh attempt to kill him, his
departure for his native Tarsus. In passing it is
worth notice that the man who lays hands on St Paul
and baptizes him is no Apostle or even evangelist,
but a simple disciple of Damascus, Ananias (ix. 17,
18). The last verse of the story (ix. 31) is this : " So
the Ecclesia throughout all Judæa and Galilee and
Samaria had peace, being built ; and walking by the
fear of the Lord and by the invocation (παράκλησις) of
the Holy Spirit (probably the invoking His guidance as
Paraclete to the Ecclesia), was multiplied." Here again
the Ecclesia has assumed a wider range. It is no longer
the Ecclesia of Jerusalem nor is it the several Ecclesiae
of Jerusalem *and* Samaria and other places. That is
language which we shall find in St Paul, but not in
the Acts, except as regards regions external to the
Holy Land. The Ecclesia was still confined to
Jewish or semi-Jewish populations and to ancient

Jewish soil; but it was no longer the Ecclesia of a
single city, and yet it was *one*: probably as corresponding, by these three modern representative
districts of Judæa, Galilee and Samaria, to the ancient
Ecclesia which had its home in the whole land of
Israel.

These limits however were soon to be crossed.
The first step takes place on a journey of St Peter
through the whole land (διερχόμενον διὰ πάντων, ix.
32), which shews that he regarded the whole as now
come within the sphere of his proper work, as it had
to all intents and purposes been within the sphere
of his work in the prelusive ministrations accompanying the Lord's own Ministry. On his way down
to the coast he is said to have come to "the saints"
or "holy ones" that dwelt at Lydda. The phrase
is a remarkable one. It has occurred once already
a few verses back (ix. 13) in Ananias's answer to the
word of the Lord spoken to him in a dream, "I
have heard concerning this man (Saul) how much
evil he did to *thy saints* at Jerusalem." Members of
the holy Ecclesia of Israel were themselves holy by
the mere fact of membership, and this prerogative
phrase is here boldly transferred to the Christians by
the bold Damascene disciple. Its use is the correlative
of the use of the term *Ecclesia*, the one relating to
individuals as members of the community, the other
to the community as a whole. It occurs once more

in the same little group of events (ix. 41), and once on St Paul's own lips in the bitterness of his self-accusation for his acts of persecution, in his defence before King Agrippa (xxvi. 10), probably in intentional repetition of Ananias's language respecting those same acts of his. It was a phrase that was likely to burn itself into his memory in that connexion. All know how commonly it occurs in the Epistles and Apocalypse, but its proper original force is not always remembered.

Then comes the story of Cornelius, the Roman Centurion in the great chiefly heathen seaport of Cæsarea, and his reception and baptism by St Peter, on the double warrant of the vision at Joppa and the outburst of the mysterious tongues while Peter was yet speaking. This was the act of Peter on his own sole responsibility, and at first it caused disquiet among some at least of the original members of the Ecclesia. We read (xi. 1) " Now the apostles and the brethren that were in Judæa (or rather perhaps, all about Judæa, κατὰ τὴν 'Ιουδαίαν) heard that the Gentiles also had received the word of God." And when Peter went up to Jerusalem they of the " circumcision " (*i.e.* probably those spoken of in x. 45, who had accompanied St Peter, for as yet there is no sign of uncircumcised believers) disputed with Peter for eating with men uncircumcised. This was apparently a complaint preferred in the presence of the

Apostles and brethren, but we hear nothing of any formal assertion of authority either by St Peter himself, or by the Apostles generally, or by the Apostles and brethren together. St Peter simply seeks to carry the whole body with him by patient explanation of the circumstances and considerations belonging to the case. And he has his reward : the objectors hold their peace (ἡσύχασαν, a word which points to the objectors) and glorify God for having given the Gentiles also repentance unto life. It was a great step that was thus taken ; but it did not lie outside the local limits of the ancient Ecclesia. Cornelius was a sojourner in the land of Israel, and moreover one of them that feared or reverenced God, as it was called, a proselyte of the less strict sort.

LECTURE IV.

THE ECCLESIA OF ANTIOCH.

The Origin of the Ecclesia.

THE pause before the local limits of the ancient Ecclesia were overstepped was of short duration. St Luke's next section tells us how fugitives from the persecution which began with Stephen had preached the word all along the Syrian coast up to Antioch, and by this time a large number of disciples had been gathered together. In other words, here was a great capital, including a huge colony of Jews, in close relations with all the Greek-speaking world and all the Syriac-speaking world; and in its midst a multitude of Christian disciples had come into existence in the most casual and unpremeditated way. No Apostle had led or founded a mission; no Apostle had taught there. But there the Christian congregation was, and its existence and future could not but be of the highest interest to the original body of Christians. What the relations would be between the two bodies was certainly not a question that could be answered off hand. " Hearing the tidings ", we read (xi. 22), " the Ecclesia which was at Jerusalem " (here once more we have a narrower title, doubtless with a view to the antithesis of Jerusalem and Antioch) "sent forth Barnabas to Antioch." Barnabas, as we know, was not one of the Twelve. Probably the Twelve themselves felt that at the present moment it might be imprudent to take part personally in the affairs of Antioch, and to put forth even the semblance of apostolic authority there. But they (and not they only but the whole Ecclesia) sent a trusted envoy whose discretion could be relied on. He came and recognised what St Luke calls " the grace that was of God " ($\tau\grave{\eta}\nu$ $\chi\acute{a}\rho\iota\nu$ $\tau\grave{\eta}\nu$ $\tauο\hat{\upsilon}$ $θεο\hat{\upsilon}$), (the repetition of the article in the true text is full of meaning), the merciful extension of the area of saving knowledge and faith, and that by a kind of instrumentality which could be referred to nothing but the Providence of God. Accordingly, as a true son of encouragement or exhortation, Barnabas exhorted ($\pi\alpha\rho\epsilon\kappa\acute{a}\lambda\epsilon\iota$) all to abide by the purpose of their heart in the Lord, and many fresh conversions were the result of his teaching. But feeling apparently that this was a work for which St Paul's experience peculiarly fitted him, he fetched him from Tarsus, and together at Antioch they spent a year. The disciples, we are told, were there first called Christians; but there is reason to believe that St Luke does not

mean that the name was assumed by themselves.
He does speak of Paul and Barnabas being "hospita-
bly received[1] *in the Ecclesia*", thereby recognising the
disciples at Antioch as forming an Ecclesia—a significant fact as regards both the recognition of this
irregularly founded community at Antioch, and the
changes in the use of the term *ecclesia* itself. Still
however it was a community of men who were in
some sense or other *Jewish* Christians: the widely
spread opinion to the contrary rests on the wrong
reading Ἕλληνας in xi. 20.

Sending help to Jerusalem.

Before long an opportunity came for a practical
exhibition of fellowship between the two communities.
The famine in Judæa led to the sending of help (εἰς
διακονίαν) by the disciples at Antioch to the brethren
in Judæa. It was sent by Barnabas and Paul, and
sent to "the elders" (xi. 30). Who were they? And
why was it not sent to the Apostles? Both questions
have been practically answered by Dr Lightfoot.
He points out[2] that St Luke's narrative of the persecution by Herod in xii. 1-19 (his vexing of certain
of them of the Ecclesia) comes in parenthetically in

---

[1] Such is the least difficult explanation of the curious word συν-
αχθῆναι as in Matt. xxv. and (with εἰς τὸν οἶκον, εἰς τὴν οἰκίαν) some
Old Testament passages; also their original *'āsăph* (*to gather*) in Ps.
xxvii. 10.

[2] *Galatians*, p. 123, n. 3, p. 126.

connexion with this mission to Jerusalem, but probably preceded it in order of time. After the murder
of James the son of Zebedee, St Peter, we are told
(xii. 17), on being delivered from prison (after prayer
being earnestly made by the Ecclesia) "went to
another place"; and it is likely enough that the
other ten did the same. It is possible that on
their departure they appointed elders to whom to
entrust the care of the Ecclesia in their absence. It is
also possible that the Ecclesia itself may have provided itself with elders when the Apostles departed.
But it is more likely that they were in office already,
and merely assumed fresh responsibilities under the
stress of circumstances. Some have even thought
that they were the Seven under another name. This
is a very improbable hypothesis. But it is at least
conceivable, supposing the Seven to have been
appointed for the Hellenists alone, that there were
already elders, and that these supposed elders at that
time chiefly represented the Hebrew part of the
community. This however is quite uncertain; nor is
it important to know. In any case it is but reasonable to suppose[1] that the Christian elders were not a
new kind of officers, but simply a repetition of the
ordinary Jewish elders, $z^e q\bar{e}n\bar{i}m$, πρεσβύτεροι, who constituted (as Dr Lightfoot says) the usual government
of the Synagogue. "Hence," he adds, "the silence of
St Luke. When he first mentions the presbyters, he

---

[1] See Lightfoot, *Philippians*, 191-3.

introduces them without preface, as though the institution were a matter of course."

The Antiochian Mission.

From this point the distinctive work of St Paul
begins, and the first stage of it has a remarkable
inauguration. At Antioch, "in the Ecclesia which was
there", there were certain prophets and teachers, five
being named, Barnabas first and Paul last. The
prophets here spoken of are probably the same,
wholly or in part, as the prophets mentioned before in
xi. 27 as having come down from Jerusalem to
Antioch, Agabus being one of them. While they are
holding some solemn service (described as λειτουρ-
γούντων τῷ κυρίῳ) and fasting, the Holy Spirit speaks,
evidently by the mouth of a prophet, "Separate me
Barnabas and Saul unto the work unto which I have
called them." The service here denoted by the verb
λειτουργέω was probably a service of prayer. The
context suggests that it was not a regular and cus-
tomary service (like "the prayer" at Jerusalem earlier,
see p. 45) but a special act of worship on the part of a
solemn meeting of the whole Ecclesia, held expressly
with reference to a project for carrying the Gospel
to the heathen. Thus the voice would seem to have
sanctioned the mission of particular men, perhaps
also even the project itself: but not to have been a
sudden call to an unexpected work. The persons

who are thus represented as doing service to the
Lord are almost certainly the prophets and teachers
mentioned just before. With fasting, prayer, and
laying on of hands, Barnabas and Saul are let go. It
is disputed whether the recipients of the prophetic
word and performers of the last-mentioned acts of mission, were the prophets and teachers, or the Ecclesia.
But on careful consideration it is difficult to doubt
that the mouthpieces of the Divine command should
be distinguished from those who have to execute it.
In other words the members of the Ecclesia itself are
bidden to set Barnabas and Saul apart; and it is the
members of the Ecclesia itself that dismiss them with
fast and prayer and laying on of hands, whether the
last act was performed by all of them, or only by
representatives of the whole body, official or other.
So also on their return they gather the Ecclesia together (xiv. 27) and report what has befallen them.

This mission is no doubt specially described as
due to a Divine monition: the setting apart comes
from the Holy Spirit (to which in all probability the
later words in xiii. 4 "being sent forth by the Holy
Ghost" refer back); but the mission is also from
the Christians of Antioch, whether directly or through
the other three prophets and teachers, since the Holy
Spirit, Himself the life and bond of every Ecclesia,
makes the Christians of Antioch His instruments for
setting Barnabas and Paul apart. It is with reference
to this mission that, as I mentioned before, St Luke

applies the name Apostles to Paul and Barnabas; and under no other circumstances does he apply the name to either of them. Thus his usage both illustrates and is illustrated by 2 Cor. viii. 23 ("apostles of churches") and Phil. ii. 25 ("your apostle," viz. Epaphroditus).

The first missionary journey.

We need not follow the details of the journey, memorable for the turning from the Jews to the Gentiles at the Pisidian Antioch, and so beginning the preaching of the Gospel to heathen Gentiles in their own land. But we must not overlook one important verse, xiv. 23. Having preached successfully at Lystra, Iconium and the Pisidian Antioch on the way out, they visit these cities again on the way home, stablishing (ἐπιστηρίζοντες) the souls of the disciples. Then " having chosen for them (χειροτονήσαντες—the confusion with χειροθεσία is much later than the Apostolic age) elders in each Ecclesia (κατ' ἐκκλησίαν), having prayed with fastings, they commended them to the Lord on whom they had believed." Here first we find that these infant communities are each called an Ecclesia, not indeed (so far as appears) from the first preaching, but at least from the second confirmatory visit. Further, Paul and Barnabas follow the precedent of Jerusalem by appointing elders in Jewish fashion (elders[1] being indeed an institution of

---

[1] Lightfoot, *Philippians* 193.

Jewish communities of the Dispersion as well as of
Judæa), and with this simple organisation they entrusted the young Ecclesiae to the Lord's care, to
pursue an independent life.   Such seems to be the
meaning of the phrase "they commended them to
the Lord on whom they had believed" (xiv. 23),
which resembles some of the farewell words spoken
to the Ephesian Elders at Miletus (xx. 32).

On their return to Antioch, "from whence", St Luke
takes care expressly to remind us—" from whence they
had been committed to the grace of God for the
work which they fulfilled ", they at once proceed to
give an account of the task entrusted to them.   They
call together the Ecclesia and relate what God had
done with them and how he had opened to the
Gentiles a door of faith.   No defence or explanation
was necessary here.   They had done what they had
been sent to do.   The turning to the Gentiles (xiii. 46)
had evidently been contemplated from the first as a
probable contingency, though the Jews were to be
addressed first.

It is hardly necessary to say that these events,
which happened about the year 50 A.D., constitute
one of the greatest epochs, perhaps the greatest,
in the history of the Ecclesia at large.   Henceforth
it was to contain members who had never in any
sense belonged to the Jewish Ecclesia.   There was
henceforth no intelligible limit for it short of universality : and thus, while it never cut itself off from its

primitive foundation, it entered on a career which imposed on it totally new conditions.

The Conference at Jerusalem.

In the steps hitherto taken the Ecclesia of Antioch had acted independently and apparently without difference of opinion. But soon a troubling of the peace came from without, from Judæa. It is worth notice that we hear nothing of complaints against the Ecclesia of Antioch as having exceeded its legitimate powers. The appeal of the envoys from Judæa was simply to the Jewish law as binding on all Christians, "Except ye be circumcised after the custom of Moses, ye cannot be saved" (xv. 1). Evidently the heathen converts made by St Paul and St Barnabas had not been circumcised, and this proceeding had been accepted by the Ecclesia of Antioch, and was evidently intended to guide their future action in regard to converts from the heathen. To act thus was to decide that Judaism was not the necessary porch of entrance into the discipleship of the Gospel, and that Gentiles might pass at once into the Christian fold without doing homage to the Jewish law, and without any obligation to future allegiance to it. It would have been surprising indeed if all the Jewish Christians of Palestine had been ready at once, either to accept this as the right course to adopt, or to acquiesce in leaving the Christians of Antioch free to pursue their own way without hindrance or remonstrance.

What view the Twelve took of the matter, we do not know. It is hardly likely that the Jewish zealots within the Ecclesia of Jerusalem would commence an agitation at Antioch in person without having first tried to induce the leading men at Jerusalem to take action. If they did so, we know that they failed: nothing can be clearer in this respect than the words of the epistle recorded further on in the chapter (xv. 24), "Forasmuch as we have heard that certain of our number (τινὲς ἐξ ἡμῶν, so the rather startling right reading, meaning doubtless 'some members of our Ecclesia')—that certain of our number troubled you with words, disturbing your souls, *to whom we gave no charge*" (οἷς οὐ διεστειλάμεθα, 'we' being the Apostles, Elders, and the whole Ecclesia). But if the Twelve and other leading men refused to abet the Judaizing zealots, it does not follow that they already were firm and clear on behalf of the policy of Antioch : later incidents render it improbable that they were. Doubtless they were not prepared to come to a final decision without taking time.

What might have easily become a schism of impassable depth was averted by the forbearance of the brethren at Antioch. The disputes between the Judaizers and Paul and Barnabas led them to send Paul and Barnabas, with others, to hold a consultation with "the Apostles and Elders" at Jerusalem. It would seem as though St Paul himself hesitated at first about going, doubtless from a fear of compro-

mising the cause which he was determined that no
Jerusalem authority should lead him to abandon. "I
went up ", he says (Gal. ii. 2), "in obedience to a revelation." The envoys set out, " speeded on their way
by the Ecclesia " (Acts xv. 3). They passed through
Phœnicia and Samaria, telling the tale of the conversion of the Gentiles, and " caused great joy to all the
brethren": to those regions the scruples of Jerusalem
had not spread. At Jerusalem " they were received
by the Ecclesia and the Apostles and the Elders ", the
three being carefully enumerated, as if to mark the
formality of the reception, and its completely representative character. Before the assembly the envoys
repeated the tale of the successful mission, and then
the gainsayers, now described as of the sect of the
Pharisees (xv. 5), rose up to maintain the necessity of
circumcision and the retention of the Law, as obligatory
on the Gentiles. Then the discussion would seem to
have been adjourned. It was probably before the
assembly met again that those private conferences
with the leading Apostles took place to which alone
St Paul makes explicit reference in his narrative in
Galatians[1].

The final assembly is described by St Luke (xv. 6)
at the outset as a gathering together of the Apostles
and the Elders to see concerning this discourse (λόγου,
practically, this matter). It can hardly be doubted
that the Ecclesia at large was in some manner like-

---

[1] See Lightfoot, *Galatians* 124 f.

wise present[1]. This follows not only from the association of "the whole Ecclesia" with the Apostles and the
Elders in the sending of a deputation to Antioch (*v.* 22),
but still more clearly from the words "and all the
multitude held their peace" in *v.* 12, since it is inconceivable that the body of Elders should be called "the
multitude.". On the other hand St Luke could hardly
have omitted to mention the Ecclesia in that initial
v. 6, unless the chief responsibility had been recognised as lying with the Apostles and the Elders.

Every one knows the order of incidents, the
opening speech by St Peter appealing to the very
similar event of his own Divinely sanctioned admission of Cornelius, and arguing against tempting God
by laying on the neck of the disciples a yoke which
neither their own Jewish fathers nor themselves had
had strength to bear; next the recital by Paul and
Barnabas of the signs and wonders by which God
had set His seal to the work among the Gentiles;
then James's renewed reference to Peter's argument,
confirmation of it from the prophecy of Amos, and
final announcement of his own opinion (διὸ ἐγὼ
κρίνω) against troubling Gentile converts, but in
favour of sending them a message (or possibly, enjoining them, ἐπιστεῖλαι) to observe four abstinences.
These need not be considered now[2]. It is enough

---

[1] So Iren. *cont. Haer.* III. xii. 14 cum...universa ecclesia convenisset
in unum.

[2] See Hort's *Judaistic Christianity*, pp. 68 ff.

to say that on the two points at issue, circumcision and the bindingness of the Jewish law, they give no support to the demands of the Judaizers. Whether the abstinences here laid down be of Jewish or even Mosaic origin or not, at most they are isolated precepts of expediency, not resting on the principle which was in dispute. And lastly we have the decision of "the apostles and the elders and all the ecclesia" to send to Antioch with Paul and Barnabas two chosen envoys from their own number, "leading men among the brethren", Judas Barsabbas and Silas, and with them a letter.

The letter and its reception.

The salutation at the head of the letter is from "the apostles and the elder brethren to the brethren who are of the Gentiles throughout Antioch and Syria and Cilicia" (such seems to be the force of κατά with a single article for the three names), the central and in every way most important, Antioch, being placed at the head, and then the rest of Syria, and the closely connected region of Cilicia. The Ecclesia is not separately mentioned in the salutation; on the other hand the unusual phrase "the elder brethren" (for such is assuredly not only the right reading but the right punctuation) indicates that they who held the office of Elder were to be regarded as bearing the characteristic from which the title itself had arisen, and were but elder brothers at the head of a great

family of brethren.   The letter, after the salutation,
begins by repudiating the agitators who had gone
down to Antioch.   Next it states that it had been
agreed in common to send back chosen men with
Barnabas and Paul, who are spoken of in emphatically warm language, with indirect recognition of
their mission as that for which they had exposed
their lives : this was in fact a deputation from Jerusalem, exactly answering to the deputation from
Antioch to Jerusalem.   Thirdly, in a fresh sentence
the letter gives the names of the two envoys (Judas
and Silas), and the exact purpose of their mission,
to repeat in person what had just been recited in
writing (τὰ αὐτά), probably also with the inclusion of
what comes next, or fourthly, " For it seemed good
to the Holy Spirit and to us to lay on you no further
burthen save these necessary things, *viz.* the four
abstinences ; from which if ye keep yourselves it
shall be well with you.   Fare ye well."

To some points involved in this letter and the
accompanying circumstances we must return just
now.   But first we should glance at the historical
sequel, under the two heads of St Luke's and St
Paul's narratives.

Paul and Barnabas 'go down' to Antioch (the
phrase is significant,—Jerusalem is still the central
height).   They gather together the multitude of the
brethren (τὸ πλῆθος) and gave them the epistle
(ἐπέδωκαν) ;   a phrase which shews that, as might

indeed be gathered from the terms of the salutation, it was to the Ecclesia at large that the letter was addressed. Having read it they rejoice at the encouragement (παρακλήσει); a vague word, it might seem, but an appropriate one: it expressed the " God speed you " (so to speak) which had been pronounced on their own work and on the conditions of freedom under which it had been begun. The effect of the letter is reinforced by the personal representatives of Jerusalem : Judas and Silas, themselves also prophets, with much discourse encouraged (or exhorted, παρεκάλεσαν) the brethren and stablished [them] (ἐπεστήριξαν). They stay some time, and then are dismissed by the brethren with peace and return to those that sent them (the ἀποστόλους of the Textus Receptus and the Authorised Version is certainly a wrong reading). Meanwhile Paul and Barnabas continue in Antioch, teaching and preaching the good tidings of the word of the Lord, along with many others also (xv. 35).

St Peter at Antioch.

Such is St Luke's account, a history of smooth water. It did not enter into his purpose to wake up the memories of an incident on which the Ecclesia had been well-nigh wrecked, but which happily had ended in a manner which enabled it to pursue its course uninjured, or rather we must suppose strengthened. Nothing, we may be sure, but the

conviction that the whole future of the Gentile
Ecclesiae was bound up in the vindication of his
own authentic Apostleship, would have induced St
Paul to commit to paper the sad story of his conflict
with St Peter. St Peter, it would seem, had after
a while followed the four envoys to Antioch. Nothing
was more natural and expedient than that he should
visit the vigorous young community in person, and
establish friendly relations on the spot. A personal
visit like this, which might once have been imprudent,
had now become expedient. At first all went well.
He carried out completely the purpose of the Jerusalem letter by associating on equal terms with the
Gentile converts; he "ate with them", just as he had
done (to the scandal of many) at Cæsarea (xi. 3).
But when certain came down from James, he withdrew
himself in fear of them of the circumcision. This
conduct St Paul plainly calls "acting a false part"
(ὑπόκρισις Gal. ii. 13), pretending to be that which he
was not: but it was shared by the rest of the Jewish
Christians at Antioch and even at length, strange to
say, by Barnabas. St Paul alone stood firm, and
rebuked St Peter to his face in the presence of them
all. To go into the various questions arising out of
this account, as I did to a certain extent two years ago[1],
would be out of the question now. What specially
concerns our own subject is that the point of principle
really at stake was, under one aspect, the question

[1] See *Judaistic Christianity*, pp. 76 ff.

whether membership of the Christian Ecclesia could be of two orders or degrees, an inner for Jewish Christians only, and an outer. The position practically taken up for a while by St Peter and his associates must not be confounded with the position taken up by the uncompromising Judaizers who had been repudiated in the letter from Jerusalem. There is not the least sign that he affected to wish to exclude heathen converts from baptism or most other Christian privileges. But he did persuade himself that, for the time at least, uncircumcised Christians should not be allowed to sit at table with circumcised; in other words that they might in a certain sense be members of the Christian brotherhood but not be recognised as full members, unless by first becoming Jews, and accepting Jewish customs as binding on them. St Paul does not tell us how the matter ended. That was unnecessary, for all the subsequent history shewed that this compromise, the fruit of timorous and untimely prudence, must have quickly collapsed, and left the policy represented by St Paul now more firmly established than before St Peter's arrival. Thus the freedom of Gentile Christian communities was assured anew in the completest form.

LECTURE V.

THE EXERCISE OF AUTHORITY.

St James and his position.

WE have already spent much time on the Jerusalem conference and letter, and its sequel. But there remain some points which concern our subject too closely to be passed over. First, about St James. This is the second of the three occasions on which his name appears in the Acts. When St Peter was released by the angel from prison, after the martyrdom of the Apostle James the brother of John, he said to the disciples assembled in the house of John Mark "Tell these things to James and to the brethren" (xii. 17). He must then have already been in some manner prominent among the disciples. As the chief among the Lord's own brethren, and one to whom the Lord vouchsafed a separate appearance after the Resurrection (1 Cor. xv. 7), doubtless the appearance to which the well-known story in the Gospel according to the Hebrews refers (Lightfoot, *Gal.* 265), and, if so, at

which his unbelief probably came to an end, he would
evidently be held in a peculiar kind of respect in the
infant Ecclesia. St Paul alone speaks of him as an
Apostle (Gal. i. 19: and probably by implication
1 Cor. xv. 7), and the contexts seem to me distinctly
to exclude that looser sense of the term referred to
before by which mere 'Apostles of Ecclesiae' were
meant, while it is hardly less clear that he did not
anticipate the later theory which made him to have
been from the first one of the Twelve. It would seem
then that, possessing as he did in an eminent degree
the primary apostolic qualification of being a witness
of the Lord's life, death and resurrection, he was at
some early time after the persecution by Herod taken
up into the place among the Twelve vacated by his
namesake. The silence of St Luke, as compared
with his explicitness about Matthias, may be due to
the fact that in this instance it was no matter of
choice, calling for all the process described in Acts i.,
but a natural result of the combination of circumstances, such as might itself well be treated as a
sufficient intimation of the Divine will. On the other
hand no Apostleship of St James is recorded or
implied by St Luke, though he three times mentions
him in a way which marks him out as, to say the
least, a leading and prominent person. But this is less
surprising than it might otherwise be, if the prominence was due to personal circumstances, which continued to operate after his admission to the Apostolate,

just as antecedently they had procured his admission
to it.   In other words, the prominence which he has
in the Acts would not be due to his having become
an Apostle : nay, his admission to that joint responsibility might rather tend to diminish any exclusiveness
of *prestige* which he may have acquired outside the
Apostolate, and so independently of it.

Was then the prominence of St James due solely
to personal qualifications and history, not to any recognised function ?   That would be too much to say.
That at the time of his death he was practically the
ruler of the Ecclesia of Jerusalem is the least open to
doubt among the particulars of the traditions current in
the Second Century about him, by whatever name we
choose to call his government ; and at least the origin
of such a position is likely to have some connexion
with the facts mentioned or implied by St Luke.
The clearest fact about him attested by the New
Testament, Acts and St Paul alike, but enormously
exaggerated at a later time, is that he was at least
more closely connected in sentiment with the more
Jewish part of the Ecclesia of Jerusalem than were
the rest of the Apostles ; and it may well be that the
veneration in which he is said to have been held at
the time of his death even by unbelieving Jews, had
its roots in an early popularity which would make
him a valuable mediator between the stiffer sort of
Hebrew Christians and the other Apostles.   Such a
passage as that just cited from St Peter's words after

his release might, taken alone, be quite sufficiently explained by purely personal prominence. So also the fact that in Gal. ii. 9 the order is "James and Cephas and John" might well be due to the fact that the adherence of James on the occasion referred to was even more significant than that of the other two, on account of his closer relations with the Jewish party. But the two other passages of the Acts are best understood as implying that he held some recognised office or function in connexion with the Ecclesia of Jerusalem : and it does not seem unlikely that on his admission to the Apostolate it was arranged that, unlike the rest, he should exercise a definite local charge. Such a charge would of necessity become more distinct and, so to speak, monarchical when the other Apostles were absent from Jerusalem. His own circumstances were unique, and the circumstances of the Ecclesia of Jerusalem were no less unique. A peculiar function founded on peculiar qualifications is what the narrative suggests.

There is nothing in St Luke's words which bears out what is often said, that St James presided over the conference at Jerusalem. If he had, it would be strange that his name should not be mentioned separately at the beginning, where we read only that "the Apostles and the Elders" were gathered together. In the decisive speeches at the end the lead is taken by St Peter, the foremost of the Twelve. After Barnabas and Paul have ended their narrative, James

takes up the word. What he says is called an *answer*
(ἀπεκρίθη Ἰάκωβος λέγων xv. 13), probably as replying
to words uttered earlier by the more Jewish section of
the assembly during the dispute mentioned in *v. 7*.
His opening words suggest that his first appeal is to
them, and that he makes it as one to whom they might
be more willing to listen than to St Paul, " Brethren
(ἄνδρες ἀδελφοί), listen to me "; he then refers to
Peter's exposition, calling him not only by his original
name, but by the strictly Hebrew form of it, Symeon,
as though to bespeak their goodwill for what Peter
had said. Then again the words which begin his
conclusion, " Wherefore my .judgement is," cannot
reasonably be understood as an authoritative judgment pronounced by himself independently: the
whole context and what is said in *v. 22* about the
actual decision makes that interpretation morally
impossible. The sense is doubtless " I for my part[1]
judge," " this is my vote " as we should say. The
point then is that, guardian though he was of the
honour of Israel in the Ecclesia, he here throws his
voice on the side of liberty. It is no objection to
this view that he says simply ἐγώ not κἀγώ : owing
to his mention of the four abstinences his proposal
could not be simply identical with that of St Peter.

[1] Wetstein *in loc.* quotes Thuc. iv. 16 for a still weaker ὡς ἐγὼ κρίνω,
explained by the scholiast as ὡς ἐγὼ νομίζω, and the same use of κρίνω
occurs elsewhere in the Acts (xiii. 46; xvi. 15; xxvi. 8): here the sense
seems to be intermediate. Cf. the old latin version of Irenæus *cont.
Haer.* III. xii. 14 'Ego secundum me iudico.'

We saw just now that he is not named at the gathering of the assembly. It is just the same afterwards: the decision is said to be made by the Apostles and the Elders with the whole Ecclesia; the letter proceeds from the Apostles and the elder brethren: apart then from these two classes he can hardly have exercised authority in this matter.

The Authority of the Jerusalem Elders and of the Twelve.

When we pass from St James to the Apostles and Elders, the question arises, "What kind of authority they here put forth over the brethren in Antioch and the surrounding region?" The answer cannot be a simple one. The letter itself at once implies an authority, and betrays an unwillingness to make a display of it. In the forefront are set anxious friendliness, courteous approval. Whatever is in any sense imperative comes after this and subsidiary to it, and is set forth as what had seemed good "to the Holy Spirit and to us", the human authority, whatever it be, being as it were appended to that which is presumed to be Divine. Further, the semblance of a command is softened off at the end into a counsel; "from which if ye keep yourselves it shall be well with you."

So again in the next chapter (xvi. 4) the phrase used, "the decrees which had been ordained of the Apostles and Elders", seems to refer back, 'the

decrees' (δόγματα) to the twice repeated ἔδοξεν of
xv. 22, 25, 'ordained' (κεκριμένα) to St James's κρίνω
in xv. 19¹. · Δόγμα in Greek (properly only what
seems, or seems good) is one of those curiously
elastic words which vary in sharpness of meaning
according to the persons to whom a thing is said
to seem good, and to the other circumstances of
the case. The dogma of an emperor or a legislative
assembly or the Amphictyonic council is a decree,
the dogma of a philosopher is what seems to him
to be true; and between these extremes are various
shades of meaning. Here the probable sense is
nearly what we should call a 'resolution', as passed
by any deliberative body, not in form imperative but
intended to have a binding force. The New Testament is not poor of words expressive of command,
ἐντέλλομαι, ἐπιτάσσω, προστάσσω, διατάσσω, διαστέλ-
λομαι and their derivatives, to say nothing of κελεύω
and παραγγέλλω : yet none of them is used. It was
in truth a delicate and difficult position, even after
the happy decision of the assembly. The independence of the Ecclesia of Antioch had to be respected,
and yet not in such a way as to encourage disregard
either of the great mother Ecclesia, or of the Lord's
own Apostles, or of the unity of the whole Christian
body. Accordingly we do not find a word of a hint

---

¹ In the later reference (xxi. 25) we have no stronger term than
ἀπεστείλαμεν (or ἐπεστείλαμεν) κρίναντες : cf. St James's κρίνω...ἐπιστεῖλαι
(xv. 19 f.).

that the Antiochians would have done better to get
sanction from Jerusalem before plunging into such
grave responsibilities. But along with the cordial
concurrence in the release of Gentile converts from
legal requirements there goes a strong expression of
opinion, more than advice and less than a command,
respecting certain salutary restraints. A certain
authority is thus implicitly claimed. There is no
evidence that it was more than a moral authority;
but that did not make it less real.

The bases of authority differ for the two bodies
united in writing to Antioch, the Elders and the
Apostles. The Elders are to all appearance the local
elders of the Ecclesia of Jerusalem. It is impossible
that, as such, they could claim any authority properly
so called over the Ecclesia of Antioch. But they had
a large voice, backed as they were by the great body
of the Ecclesia of Jerusalem, in saying whether the
Ecclesia of Jerusalem would accept the brethren at
Antioch, and specially the Gentile converts among
them, as true brethren of their own, and true disciples
of Jesus Christ. There is no making of formal conditions of fellowship, but the Elders, as taking the
lead in making so great a concession on the part of
Jerusalem, might well feel that they had a right to
expect that the four restraints which had been set
forth would be accepted. Such a deference on the
part of Antioch would be the more proper since Paul

and Barnabas, the representatives of Antioch, had evidently accepted the resolution as a whole (see their conduct in xvi. 4).

The authority of the Apostles was of a different kind. There is indeed, as we have seen, no trace in Scripture of a formal commission of authority for government from Christ Himself. Their commission was to be witnesses of Himself, and to bear that witness by preaching and by healing. But it is inconceivable that the moral authority with which they were thus clothed, and the uniqueness of their position and personal qualifications, should not in all these years have been accumulating upon them by the spontaneous homage of the Christians of Judæa an ill-defined but lofty authority in matters of government and adminis- tration; of which indeed we have already had an instance in the laying of the price of the sold proper- ties at their feet. What is not so easy to find out is the extent to which an apostolic authority of this kind is likely to have been felt and acknowledged beyond the limits of the Holy Land. On the one hand all Christian discipleship, wherever it sprang up, must have come directly or indirectly from the central community at Jerusalem, and it is difficult to see any form the Gospel could take in transmission in which the place of the still living Apostles would not be a primary one. On the other hand we cannot forget that it was of James and Peter and John that St Paul wrote those guarded but far-reaching words (Gal. ii. 6)

" but from those who were reputed to be somewhat—
(of whatsoever sort (ὁποῖοι) they were, it maketh no
matter to me : God accepteth not a man's person)
they, I say, who were of repute imparted nothing (or
nothing farther) to me (ἐμοὶ οὐδὲν προσανέθεντο)": words
which shew that with all his unfailing anxiety to have
the concurrence of the Twelve, and not of them only
but of the Ecclesia of Jerusalem at large, he was not
prepared to obey if the Twelve had insisted on the
requirement of circumcision and the Law. Hence in
the letter sent to Antioch the authority even of the
Apostles, notwithstanding the fact that unlike the
Jerusalem elders they exercised a function towards
all Christians, was moral rather than formal ; a claim
to deference rather than a right to be obeyed.

The Twelve and the Gentiles.

In this connexion there is special force in that
familiar statement by St Paul in the context just
referred to (Gal. ii. 7–12), "when they saw that I had
been entrusted with the Gospel of the uncircumcision,
even as Peter with (a Gospel) of the circumcision
(Πέτρος τῆς περιτομῆς, not τὸ τῆς), for He that wrought
by Peter (that seems to be the sense of ὁ ἐνεργήσας
Πέτρῳ, rather than either "in Peter" or "for Peter")
unto an Apostleship (no τήν) of the circumcision (τῆς
περιτομῆς) wrought by me also unto (or for, εἰς) the
Gentiles :—and when they perceived (γνόντες) the
grace that was given unto me, James and Cephas and

John, they who were reputed to be pillars, gave to me and Barnabas right hands of fellowship (κοινωνίας), that *we* (should be, or should go; no verb) unto the Gentiles, and themselves unto the circumcision : only *they would* that we should remember the poor (*i.e.* poor Christians of Palestine); which I also for this very reason took pains to do."

Our familiarity with the idea of St Paul as the Apostle of the Gentiles makes us in reading slide over this arrangement as though it were the obvious thing to be done. In one sense it was: but what is its relation to the universal mission of the Twelve? Was it indeed to the circumcision only that our Lord had appointed them to bear witness of Himself by word and act? It is difficult to think so when we read of words which He spoke between the Resurrection and the Ascension. Those other words about the twelve thrones, and about not having gone through the cities of Israel, doubtless remained, not abrogated. But in some sense or other the twelve Apostles were surely to be for the Gentiles as well as for the old Israel; not merely through the Ecclesia which was founded on them, but in themselves. They had a relation to the ideal twelve tribes of the new Israel as well as to those of the old, which long before the time of the Christian era had become hardly less ideal.

Here comes in the purely historical question. Had the Twelve or any of them preached beyond the limits of Palestine up to this time? High authorities give this extension to St Luke's simple if vague words about St Peter after his deliverance from prison, how he " went out (*i.e.* out of John Mark's house at Jerusalem) and went his way unto another place" (xii. 17). About twelve years are said to have then elapsed since the Ascension, and reference is made to one of the traditions current in the Second Century, to the effect that our Lord had bidden the Apostles go forth into the world after twelve years. There is, however, nothing connected with the tradition which gives it substantially more weight than the other fictions about the Apostles which soon flourished luxuriantly and in endless contradictions to each other. The omission of such a cardinal event from St Luke's narrative is, I think, inconceivable; and his whole story of the doings of the Ecclesia of Antioch and St Paul's first mission becomes unintelligible if similar missionary journeys of Apostles had preceded. We must, I think, conclude that up to the date of the great conference the Twelve had not believed themselves to have received any clear Divine intimation that the time was come for them to go forth in person among the nations.

But now, independently of any action on their own part, the whole horizon was changed by the action of the Ecclesia of Antioch and the labours of Paul and Barnabas. It was no merely human series of acts which came before them for recognition. They doubtless accepted the mission from Antioch

as proceeding in the first instance from the Holy
Spirit speaking by the mouth of prophets, and as
subsequently sanctioned from heaven by the signs
and wonders which Paul and Barnabas were enabled
to work.   Here then at last the Divine monition
to themselves had come, though probably in an
unexpected form.   In the person of St Paul, long
since welcomed by themselves as a fellow-worker,
God had now raised up a mighty herald of the Gospel
for the Gentiles.   He was no delegate of theirs: his
commission was direct: but by recognising him as
specially called to do apostolic work among the
Gentiles, they were enabled to feel that by agreement
and fellowship with him they were in effect carrying
out through him that extension of their sphere which
it is incredible that they should ever have dismissed
from their minds; and meanwhile they were themselves able without misgiving to continue their work
in the narrower sphere in which they had already
laboured so long.   Whether this limitation was at
the time contemplated as permanent or as temporary,
we have of course no means of knowing: but indeed
there was no need to decide; in the future, no less
than in the present, the needful guidance was to be
looked for from heaven.   In any case this agreement
with St Paul, made in private conference, must be
kept in mind when we are reading the epistle to
Antioch which was agreed to and written so shortly
after.   They remarkably supplement each other.   On

the one hand the Twelve could not have so written had they meant henceforth to hold themselves discharged from every kind of responsibility towards Gentile Christians generally : on the other the agreement with St Paul and St Barnabas excluded them for the present from working personally among the Gentiles.

It must be noticed that the limit drawn is religious, not geographical : it is between the circumcision and the Gentiles, not between the land of Israel and Gentile lands. Thus St James was still acting quite according to the agreement when, while remaining at the head of the Ecclesia of Jerusalem, he wrote an Epistle to Jewish Christians of the Dispersion. But we hear nothing of evangelistic journeys by the Twelve for preaching to the *Jews* of heathen cities ; and it is most unlikely that any such were made. The distribution of fields of work involved in the agreement itself passed away in due time by the force of circumstances: we know of at least three of the Twelve who can be shown on trustworthy evidence to have laboured eventually in heathen lands. But that lies outside the Acts.

It is worthy of notice that we have now reached the last appearance of the Apostles collectively, or of any one of them except St James, in St Luke's narrative. His remaining chapters are wholly silent about them. By this time the work which most characteristically belonged to them, their special con-

tribution to the building up of the Ecclesia, though
not yet ended, was not henceforth to present new
features. What remained of their work in Palestine
would be a continuation of such work as St Luke
had already described. On them the Ecclesia of
the mother city had been built.

The government of the Ecclesia of Antioch.

One other supplementary observation should be
made before we leave this fifteenth chapter. In all
that we read there and previously about the young
Ecclesia of Antioch we learn absolutely nothing about
its government or administration. The prophets and
teachers have, as such, nothing to do with functions of
this kind. Doubtless a man like Barnabas, coming as
an envoy of the Ecclesia of Jerusalem (so, not simply
of the Apostles, xi. 22) and shewing such sympathy
with the local conditions of things, would acquire by
the mere force of circumstances a considerable moral
authority ; and this would presently be shared with
St Paul, when he too had come out of his Cilician retire-
ment. Of course by its very nature this position was
temporary as well as informal. Strange to say, we
hear nothing about Elders. Since we know that the
Ecclesia of Jerusalem had long had Elders, and St Paul
on returning from his first journey in Asia Minor had
appointed Elders for each local Ecclesia, it is hardly
credible that they were wanting at Antioch, to say
nothing of the influence of the precedent of the great

Jewish population. But in the Acts we hear only of "the brethren" (xv. 1, 32, 33) or "the disciples" (xi. 26, 29; xiv. 28) or "the multitude" (xv. 30) or "the ecclesia" (xi. 26; xiii. 1; xiv. 27). Evidently at this time the general body of disciples at Antioch must have taken at least a large share in the acts of the Christian community.

LECTURE VI.

ST PAUL AT EPHESUS.

The later history of the resolutions of the conference.

THE rest of the Acts need not occupy us long
After certain days Paul said unto Barnabas " Let us
return now and visit the brethren in every city
wherein we proclaimed the word of the Lord, and see
how they fare." This journey then proceeded from
no act of the Ecclesia of Antioch nor (so far as
appears) from a special Divine monition. It was
apparently in intention, and certainly as regards the
first part of it, merely supplementary to the former
journey. As we know, St Paul and Barnabas had a
division of opinion, and separated, Paul taking Silas,
one of the envoys of the Ecclesia of Jerusalem, and
himself a prophet. At Lystra a still more important
fellow-labourer was added to his company in the
person of Timothy, whom for prudential reasons he
circumcised; doubtless because, though hitherto form-

ally outside the old covenant, he had been from childhood to all intents and purposes a Jew[1]. As they went
through the cities they delivered to them (masculine:
to the disciples there) the resolutions which had been
decided on (τὰ δόγματα τὰ κεκριμένα) by the Apostles
and Elders that were at Jerusalem. The region through
which they were now travelling had nothing to do
with the provinces associated with Antioch, *viz.*
Syria and Cilicia, to which the Jerusalem letter had
been addressed. But the conversions which had taken
place in that very region formed the first link in the
chain of circumstances which led to the writing of the
letter: and if the Ecclesia of Antioch were to accept
loyally the restraints on neophytes imposed by the
letter, it was impossible that their missionary, on now
at once revisiting the scene of his mission, should fail
to press these requirements upon his converts. But
(with the exception of an allusion by St James or
the Jerusalem Elders in xxi. 25) this is the last
that we hear of these requirements in the Acts,
and St Paul in his Epistles makes no allusion to them
directly or indirectly. It is of course possible that
St Luke's silence on this point for the rest of this
journey, and for all the subsequent journeyings, was
not intended to be expressive. He *may* have wished
the single instance given at the outset to be understood as carried on through the rest of his narrative.
But the manner in which the one statement is made

---

[1] See *Judaistic Christianity*, pp. 84 ff.

does not suggest such an extension; nor is it likely that St Luke would have failed to repeat it for at least one region now first entered on, had he wished it to be carried forward by his readers. But St Paul's own silence is more significant still. The truth probably is that he accepted the four restraints appended to the main purpose of the letter, but did not really care for them, preferring to seek the same ends by other means; and so that he did not attempt to enforce them with respect to Christian converts for which the Ecclesia of Antioch was in no sense responsible; having perhaps already found reason in Lycaonia to doubt their expediency, though, faithful to his trust, he introduced them *there.* At all events the great liberative measure to which the Apostles joined with the Elders and Ecclesia of Jerusalem in setting their hands stood fast, and determined the character of by far the greater part of the new Ecclesia, while these petty adjuncts to it, having served their purpose, dropped away, though many in ancient, and even in modern times, have tried to persuade themselves that they are still binding on all Christians.

The next verse to that which we have now been examining tells us simply that "the Ecclesiae (*i.e.* the congregations of the Lycaonian region) were strengthened (or solidified, ἐστερεοῦντο) by their faith, and multiplied in number daily" (xvi. 5). This is the last time that the word ἐκκλησία is used by St Luke, except for that of Jerusalem and in the peculiar case of the Ephesian Elders at Miletus.

How St Paul and his companions came to extend their journey beyond Lycaonia, we are not told. When they had passed through Phrygia and Galatia and reached Alexandria Troas the vision of the Macedonian beckoned them across the Hellespont, and so they entered Europe. As everyone will remember, the chief places of their preaching were Philippi, Thessalonica, Berœa, Athens, Corinth. Not a word here of Ecclesiae, for the Christian communities were only in their earliest stage of existence.

The founding of the Ecclesia of Ephesus.

On his way back to the east St Paul diverged rapidly from his course to snatch a visit to Ephesus, where he dropped Priscilla and Aquila, and there he began to argue with the Jews in the synagogue, but quickly took leave. If, as the following narratives suggest, this was the beginning of Ephesian Christianity, it is much to be remembered as a *bona fide* instance of a great central capital which could legitimately claim an Apostle as the founder of its Christian community. It will be remembered that shortly after leaving Lycaonia, Paul and his friends are said to have been " hindered by the Holy Spirit from speaking the word in Asia," *i.e.* Proconsular Asia ; which implies that personally they (or Paul) had been desiring to

preach there, and doubtless specially in Ephesus.
The deferred wish was now to be fulfilled, though
still, so to speak, only in a representative manner, for
there was no time for effectual preaching. Promising
to return if God will, St Paul hurries across the
Mediterranean to Cæsarea, goes up to Jerusalem and
greets the Ecclesia there (here simply called τὴν ἐκκλησίαν, Jerusalem itself being indicated only by the
word ἀναβάς 'goes up'), and then returns to Antioch
for some time; he sets out afresh through Phrygia and
Galatia, "stablishing all the disciples" made on his
last journey, and so at last reaches Ephesus in good
earnest and makes a long stay, in which he becomes
the founder of Christian Ephesus in very deed.

One early incident of this stay is mentioned which
specially concerns us. After St Paul had been
preaching and arguing in the synagogue for the space
of three months, when at length some of the Jews
become hardened in disbelief and publicly revile
'the Way,' he forms a separate congregation of the
disciples, probably Jewish Christians and Gentile
Christians alike, and carries on his public disputations
in what was probably a neutral building, the σχολή
or 'lecture hall' of Tyrannus.

The period of from two to three years then spent
at Ephesus and in the surrounding region was full of
dangers and troubles, of which the Epistles alone
afford us some glimpses. They mark St Paul's
anxiety to build up carefully and solidly the Ecclesiae

of the most important region of that great peninsula now called Asia Minor, which he had in a manner made peculiarly his own, and which from childhood must have had a special interest for him from the proximity of Tarsus to the Cilician Gates, the pass by which the greater part of the peninsula was entered from the south. The last incident of that period mentioned by St Luke brings us face to face with another sort of Ecclesia from those whose origin we have been tracing. He employs the word ἐκκλησία not only for the regular assembly of the Ephesian people (xix. 39), but, by a very unusual way of speaking, for the tumultuous gathering on behalf of the Ephesian goddess (xix. 32, 41). Before that last incident St Paul had meditated a fresh journey of great length, first a visit to the European Christian communities founded by him on his former westward journey, then to Jerusalem once more, where he wished to find himself at Pentecost, the great national festival, and lastly to Rome (xix. 21).

St Paul's discourse to the Ephesian Elders at Miletus.

The incidents of the journey, with one important exception, do not concern our purpose. Anxiety not to spend time in Proconsular Asia made St Paul refrain from going back to Ephesus on his way to Palestine. But, touching at Miletus, he thence, we are told, "sent to Ephesus and called to him the

Elders of the Ecclesia." St Luke speaks of them
simply thus, as though no further explanation were
needed. We have seen already how St Paul instituted an administration by Elders in the smaller
Ecclesiae which he founded in Lycaonia, and it is but
natural to conclude that he would pursue the same
plan elsewhere. Whether the institution took place
at an early date in his long stay (so that they would
be acting along with and under him), or took place
only on his departure, as seems best to suit the
former precedent, we have no means of knowing.
Superficially it might seem as if the early verses
of his address favoured the first mentioned view,
but in reality they are neutral, what is there said
of the Elders' knowledge of St Paul's acts and
teaching from the day of his arrival being, to say
the least, addressed to them in their character of
Christian disciples, not of Christian Elders. More
is contained in xx. 28, partly about the Elders of
the Ecclesia, partly about the Ecclesia itself. "Take
heed to yourselves and to all the flock, in which the
Holy Spirit set you as ἐπισκόπους."

First, how are we to understand this last word?
No one, I suppose, doubts now that the persons
meant are those first mentioned as "Elders of the
Ecclesia." Have we then here a second title? The
only tangible reasons for thinking so (apart from
certain passages in Philippians and the Pastoral
Epistles, which must presently be considered) are that

in the Second Century the word was certainly used as
a title, though for a different office; and that it was
already in various use as a title in the Greek world.
But against this we must set the fact that both in the
Bible (LXX., Apocrypha, and the New Testament
itself, I Pet. ii. 25) and in other literature (including
Philo) it retains its common etymological or descriptive meaning 'overseer', and this meaning alone gives
a clear sense here. The best rendering would I
think be, "in which the Holy Spirit set you to have
oversight", the force being distinctly predicative. We
shall have, as I said just now, to consider the word
again in connexion with Philippians and the Pastoral
Epistles, but for the present we had better remain
at Miletus or rather Ephesus.

Secondly, the Elders are said to have been set
in the flock of Ephesus to have oversight of it *by the
Holy Spirit.* Neither here nor anywhere else in the
address is there any indication that St Paul himself
had had anything to do with their appointment,
the contrast in this to the Pastoral Epistles being
very remarkable. It is no doubt conceivable that he
might describe such an act of his own as coming
from the Holy Spirit: but apart from prophetic
monitions, of which there is no trace here, it would
be hard to find another example[1].

Again, it is conceivable that this language might
be used without any reference to the mode of ap-

---

[1] I Cor. vii. 40 is obviously quite different.

pointment, the Holy Spirit being regarded simply as, so to speak, the author of all order.

But the manner in which the Holy Spirit is elsewhere associated with joint acts, acts involving fellowship, suggests that here the appointment came from the Ecclesia itself. Doubtless, as far as we can tell, such was not the case in those Lycaonian communities where (outside of Palestine) we first read of the appointment of Elders. But the case of comparatively small communities, recently formed and rapidly visited, might well induce St Paul in the first instance to start them with Elders of his own choice: while in such a capital as Ephesus, having probably already made a long stay there, he might well think the Ecclesia ripe for the responsibility. In so doing he would be practically following the precedent set at Jerusalem in the case of the Seven (vi. 3–6). In that case the appointment of the Seven was sealed, so to speak, by the Apostles praying and laying hands of blessing on the Seven; and so it may well have been here.

Thirdly, the function of the Elders is described in pastoral language ('take heed to...the flock,' 'tend,' 'wolves...not sparing the flock'). Such language, as we might expect, was probably not unknown as applied to Jewish elders. Apparently[1] (though not

[1] See the passages in Levy and Fleischer's *Lex.* iv. 120 f. The Aramaic verb (used only for men) is פַּרְנֵם, the substantive פַּרְנָס, the sense like that of the biblical רָעָה, including the sense of tending or leading and feeding.

quite clearly) it is applied in the Talmud to them as well as to other guides and rulers. But it was impossible that this aspect of the office should not assume greater weight, under the circumstances of a Christian Ecclesia. The unique redemption to which the Ecclesia owed its existence involved the deepening and enlarging of every responsibility, and the filling out what might have been mere administration with spiritual aims and forces. But the precise form which the work of the Elders was to take is not clearly expressed. The side of shepherding most expressed by 'tending' ($\pi o\iota\mu a\acute{\iota}\nu\omega$) is government and guidance rather than feeding[1]; nor is there any other distinct reference to teaching, the two imperatives being "take heed to yourselves and to the flock," and "watch ye" or "be wakeful" ($\gamma\rho\eta\gamma o\rho\epsilon\hat{\iota}\tau\epsilon$ xx. 31), spoken with reference to the double danger of grievous wolves from without, and men speaking perverse things from within. But this 'watching' does indirectly seem to involve teaching, public or private, in virtue of the words which follow, "remembering that for a space of three years night and day I ceased not to admonish each one," the practical form taken by the Apostle's vigilance being thus recalled to mind as needing to be in some way carried on by themselves. Moreover it is hard to see how the work of tending and protection could be performed

[1] See John xxi. 16 where 'tending' ($\pi o\acute{\iota}\mu a\iota\nu e$) is contrasted with 'feeding' ($\beta\acute{o}\sigma\kappa e$) both in the preceding and in the following verse.

without teaching, which indeed would itself be a
necessary part of the daily life of a Christian, as of a
Jewish community; and it does not appear by whom
it was to be carried on mainly and regularly if not by
the Elders, or at least by some of them. No other
office in the Ecclesia of Ephesus is referred to in
the address.

Next for the Ecclesia of Ephesus itself.

Early in the term we had occasion to notice
the significance of this phrase "the Ecclesia of God
which He purchased by the blood of His own," as
joining on the new society of Christ's disciples to the
ancient Ecclesia of Israel, and marking how the idea of
the sacrificial redemption wrought by the Crucified
Messiah, succeeding to the Paschal redemption of
the Exodus, was bound up in the idea of the Christian
Ecclesia. Here we evidently are carried into a loftier
region than any previous use of the word *Ecclesia* in
the Acts would obviously point to. This language
was but natural, since the words then spoken were
then supposed to be last words. They are part of
St Paul's solemn farewell to the cherished Ecclesia
of his own founding. He begins with the actual
circumstances of the moment, the local Ephesian community, which was the flock committed to the Ephesian
Elders, and then goes on to say that that little flock
had a right to believe itself to be the Ecclesia of God
which He had purchased to be His own possession
at so unspeakable a price. Of course in strictness

the words belong only to the one universal Christian
Ecclesia: but here they are transferred to the individual Ecclesia of Ephesus, which alone these Elders
were charged to shepherd.   In the Epistles we shall
find similar investment of parts of the universal
Ecclesia with the high attributes of the whole.   This
transference is no mere figure of speech.   Each
partial society is set forth as having a unity of its
own, and being itself a body made up of many
members has therefore a corporate life of its own:
and yet these attributes could not be ascribed to it as
an absolutely independent and as it were insular
society: they belong to it only as a representative
member of the great whole[1].

In xx. 32, which follows the calling to mind of
St Paul's own former admonitions, he commends the
Elders "to the Lord and to the word of His grace",
just as he and Barnabas, on leaving the Lycaonian
churches with their newly appointed Elders, had
commended them to 'the Lord on whom they had
believed' (xiv. 23).   "The word of His grace" here
is what is called in *v.* 24 "the Gospel of the grace of
God", doubtless with special reference to the grace
by which Gentiles were admitted into covenant with
God.   Firm adherence to that Gospel would be the

---

[1] The phrase '*Ecclesia of God*,' which we find here, adopted and
adapted as we have seen from the Old Testament, has a similar local
reference at the head of both the Epistles to the Corinthians as also in
1 Tim. iii. 5, not to speak of 1 Cor. x. 32 ; xi. 22, where, as we shall
see [p. 117], the phrase appears to have a double reference.

most essential principle to guide them, after his departure, in their faith in God.

Then he adds words which define for the future the two provinces of activity for the Ecclesia, its action within and its action without, 'building up' and 'enlargement.' The word of God's grace, he says, is indeed able[1] to build up[2], to build up the Ecclesia and each individual member thereof within (cf. ix. 31), and likewise to bestow on those who had it not already the inheritance[3] among all the sanctified, all the saints of the covenant.

His last words are a gentle and disguised warning, again with reference to his own practice, against the coveting of earthly good things, and in favour of earning by personal labour not only the supply of personal needs but the means of helping those who have not themselves the strength to labour. These are words that might well be addressed to the whole Ecclesia : but there is no turn of language to indicate a change from the address to the elders ; and various passages in the Epistles confirm the *prima facie* impression that it is to them in the first instance that the warning is addressed.

He ends with the saying of the Lord Jesus, or (it may be) the summing up of many words of His, " Happy is it rather to give than to receive."

---

[1] τῷ δυναμένῳ assuredly goes, as the Greek suggests, with λόγῳ, not with κυρίῳ (or θεῷ).

[2] No accusative, that the reference may be perfectly general.

[3] See especially xxvi. 18 ; Eph. i. 18 ; Col. i. 12.

St Paul's reception at Jerusalem and at Rome.

We may pass over the journey to Jerusalem with all its warnings of danger. At Jerusalem Paul and his company were joyfully received by "the brethren" however widely or narrowly the term should be limited in this context. Next day they went in to James, and all the Elders were present. Of the other Apostles we hear nothing. In all probability they were in some other part of Palestine. James clearly here has an authoritative position. The presence of all the Elders shews that the visit was a formal one, a visit to the recognised authorities of the Ecclesia of Jerusalem, and the primary recipient is James, the elders being only spoken of as present. On the other hand not a word is distinctly said of any act or saying of James separately. After St Paul has finished his narrative, "they" (we are told, with a vague inclusive plural) "glorified God and said to him... (xxi. 20)." Not improbably James was the spokesman: but if so, he spoke the mind of the rest. Deeply interesting as this address was, the only point which concerns us is the final reference to the letter sent to Antioch. "But as touching the Gentiles which have believed, we ourselves (ἡμεῖς) sent (or wrote, or enjoined) judging that they should beware of what is offered to idols, etc." This is said in marked contrast to the suggestion that St Paul should manifest by his own example his loyalty to the Law in the case of

born Jews. It was in effect saying that his different
teaching respecting Gentiles was what they of Jerusalem could not condemn, seeing they had themselves
sanctioned for the Gentiles only certain definite
restraints which did not involve obedience to the
Law. This accounts for the general form 'the
Gentiles which have believed'. To refer to Antioch
and Syria and Cilicia would have been irrelevant;
and moreover the regions actually addressed were
the only regions which at the time of the letter contained definitely formed Ecclesiae.

This is practically the end of the evidence de-
ducible from the Acts. After this one scene on the
second day at Jerusalem, James and the Elders
disappear from view, as the other Apostles had
disappeared long before. All that happened at
Jerusalem, at Cæsarea, and on the voyage to Rome
lies outside our subject. We hear of 'brethren' at
Puteoli and at Rome, but the word Ecclesia is not
used. The breach with the unbelieving Jews at
Rome recalls that at the Pisidian Antioch, and ends
with a similar setting forth of the Gentile reception of
the Gospel, making up for the Jewish hardness of
heart. Beginning at Jerusalem, the centre of ancient
Israel and the home of the first Christian Ecclesia, the
book points forward to a time when the centre of the
heathen world will *as such* be for a time the centre of
the Ecclesia of God.

LECTURE VII.

THE 'ECCLESIA' IN THE EPISTLES.

The uses of the word.

THUS far we have followed St Luke's narrative, with scarcely any divergence into the illustrative matter to be found in the Epistles. The Epistles however contain much important evidence of various kinds, while they also sometimes fail us in respect of information which we perhaps might have expected to find, and certainly should be glad to find. Much of the evidence will be best considered under the several Epistles successively : but, in beginning with the uses of the word *Ecclesia* itself, we shall find it clearer to take them in groups.

Everyone must have noticed St Paul's fondness for adding τοῦ θεοῦ to ἐκκλησία, "the Ecclesia (or Ecclesiae) of God". We saw just now the significance of the phrase in the adaptation of Ps. lxxiv. 2 by St Paul in addressing the Ephesian elders, as claiming for the community of Christians the prerogatives of

God's ancient Ecclesia. With the exception however of two places in 1 Tim. (iii. 5, 15), where the old name is used with a special force derived from the context, this name is confined to St Paul's earlier epistles, the two to the Thessalonians, the two to the Corinthians, and Galatians. It is very striking that at this time, when his antagonism to the Judaizers was at its hottest, he never for a moment set a new Ecclesia against the old, an Ecclesia of Jesus or even an Ecclesia of the Christ against the Ecclesia of God, but implicitly taught his heathen converts to believe that the body into which they had been baptized was itself the Ecclesia of God. This addition of τοῦ θεοῦ occurs in several of the groups of passages. Naturally, and with special force, it stands in two out of three of the places in which the original Ecclesia of Judæa is meant, and is spoken of as the object of St Paul's persecution. But more significant is the application to single Ecclesiae (the various Ecclesiae of Judæa 1 Thes. ii. 14; or Corinth 1 Cor. i. 2; 2 Cor. i. 1); or to the sum total of all separate Ecclesiae (2 Thes. i. 4; 1 Cor. xi. 16); or lastly to the one universal Ecclesia as represented in a local Ecclesia (1 Cor. x. 32; xi. 22).

On the other hand, that second aspect of the Ecclesia of God under the new Covenant, by which it is also the Ecclesia of Christ (as He Himself said "I will build *my* Ecclesia") is likewise reflected in the Epistles. The most obvious instances are the two

passages in which the Ecclesiae of Judæa are referred
to. "Ye, brethren," St Paul writes to the Thessalonians (1 Thes. ii. 14) "became imitators of the
Ecclesiae of God which are in Judæa in Christ Jesus"
(viz. by suffering like them for conscience sake).
They were Ecclesiae of God, but their distinguishing
feature was that they were "in Christ Jesus", having
their existence in Jesus as Messiah. It is as though
he shrank from altogether refusing the name 'Ecclesiae
of God' to the various purely Jewish communities
throughout the Holy Land. The next verses (1 Thes.
ii. 15, 16) contain the most vehement of all St Paul's
language against the Jews: but these are the individual
men, the perverse generation; and for their misdeeds
the Jewish Ecclesia would not necessarily as yet be
responsible, the nation's final refusal of its Messiah
not having yet come. But, apart from this possible
or even probable latent distinction, the Christian
Ecclesiae of God would be emphatically Ecclesiae of
God in Christ Jesus, He in His glorification being the
fundamental bond of Christian fellowship. The other
passage which mentions these Judæan Ecclesiae is
Gal. i. 22, "and I continued unknown to the Ecclesiae
of Judæa that are in Christ": the phrase here is
briefer, but the added ταῖς ἐν Χριστῷ gives the characteristic touch. Echoes of these two clear passages
occur with reference to other Ecclesiae. That of the
Thessalonians is in both Epistles said to be "in God
the (or our) Father and the Lord Jesus Christ". The

men of Corinth are said to be "hallowed in Christ
Jesus" (i.e. brought into the state of 'saints' in Him).
The men of Philippi "saints in Christ Jesus". The
men of Ephesus "saints and faithful in Christ Jesus";
and so the men of Colossae "saints and faithful brethren in Christ". And for the men of Rome also
there is the analogous statement (i. 6) "among whom
are ye also, *called* of Jesus Christ."

With these forms of speech we may probably
associate the difficult and unique phrase of Rom.
xvi. 16, "All the Ecclesiae of the Christ salute you."
This is the one place in the New Testament, apart
from our Lord's words to Peter, where we read of
"Ecclesiae of Christ" (or "of the Christ"), not "of
God": for the singular number we have no example.
The sense which first suggests itself, "all Christian
Ecclesiae" is very difficult to understand. That all
the Ecclesiae of not only Palestine, but Syria,
various provinces of Asia Minor, Macedonia and
Greece should have recently, either simultaneously
or by joint action, have asked St Paul to convey
their greetings to the Roman Christians is barely
credible, and the addition of πᾶσαι (omitted only in
the later Syrian text and by no version) clinches
the difficulty[1]. Observing this difficulty (which in-

---

[1] 1 Cor. xvi. 19, 20 is no true parallel, for such joint action of the
Ecclesiae (or principal Ecclesiae,—there is no πᾶσαι) of Proconsular
Asia would be quite possible, and the second phrase (*v.* 20) "all the
brethren" must by analogy mean all the individual brethren in the
midst of whom St Paul was writing from Ephesus the capital.

deed had evidently been felt long ago by Origen), some of the older commentators suppose some such limitation as "all the Ecclesiae of Greece": but this the Greek cannot possibly bear. It seems far more probable that by "the Ecclesiae of the Christ" the Messiah, St Paul means the Ecclesiae of those "of whom as concerning the flesh the Messiah came" (Rom. ix. 5), and to whom His Messiahship could not but mean more than it did to Jews of the Dispersion, much less to men of Gentile birth: in a word that he means the Ecclesiae of Judæa, of whom as we have seen, he has twice spoken already in other epistles. It might easily be that all these had been represented at some recent gathering at Jerusalem, and had there united in a message which some Jerusalem colleague or friend had since conveyed to him.

This supposition gains in probability when we notice that, whatever may be the case elsewhere, ὁ χριστὸς is never used in this Epistle without some reference to Messiahship, though not always quite on the surface[1]. The least obvious, but for our purpose the most interesting, is xiv. 18, where the whole stress lies on ἐν τούτῳ (cf. 2 Cor. xi. 13 f., 22 f.), and the mode of service of the Messiah just described is implicitly contrasted with a pretended service of the Messiah. The significance of the phrase comes out when it occurs again in that curious guarded postscript

---

[1] See Rom. vii. 4; ix. 3, 5; xv. 3 and 7 taken together.

against the Judaizers which St Paul adds after his greetings (xvi. 17–20). "Such men," he says, "serve not the Christ who is our Lord, but their own belly" (i.e. by insisting on legal distinctions of meats), while, he means to say, they pretend to be the only true servants of the Messiah. Now the salutation immediately preceding this warning contains the words which we are considering. To you, Romans, he seems to say, I am bidden to send the greetings of all the true Ecclesiae of the Messiah. But you need to be warned about some who may hereafter come troubling you, and falsely claiming to be Messiah's only faithful servants, as against me and mine. Thus the enigmatic form of the salutation may arise out of the inevitably enigmatic form of the coming warning.

Individuals not lost in the Society.

Another interesting point which it is convenient to notice here is that twofold aspect of an Ecclesia which came before us early in the Acts, as being on the one hand itself a single body, and on the other made up of single living men. Here too there is an interesting sequence, though not a perfect one, in the order of the Epistles.

The salutation to 1 and 2 Thessalonians is simply to the Ecclesia of the Thessalonians in God [our] Father and the Lord Jesus Christ (this last phrase, we may note in passing, may be considered to include the τοῦ θεοῦ of 1 and 2 Corinthians).

In 1 Cor. i. 2 on the other hand we find the two aspects coupled together by a bold disregard of grammar τῇ ἐκκλησίᾳ τοῦ θεοῦ τῇ οὔσῃ ἐν Κορίνθῳ, ἡγιασμένοις ἐν Χριστῷ Ἰησοῦ, κλητοῖς ἁγίοις : the single Ecclesia in Corinth is identical with men who have been hallowed in Christ Jesus, and called to be saints.

In 2 Cor. i. 1 there is a seeming return to the form used to the Thessalonians, the reason probably being that the name 'saints' was reserved for the following σὺν τοῖς ἁγίοις πᾶσιν τοῖς οὖσιν ἐν ὅλῃ τῇ Ἀχαίᾳ (only partially parallel to the σὺν πᾶσιν etc. of 1 Corinthians) : there may also be a distinction between the single Ecclesia of the great city Corinth and the scattered saints or Christians of the rest of Achaia.

The case of Galatians is peculiar. Here St Paul was writing, not to a city alone, or to a great city, the capital of a region, but to a region containing various unnamed cities. He writes simply to "the Ecclesiae" (plural) of Galatia : to attach to this feminine plural a masculine plural would have been awkward and puzzling (in Acts xvi. 4 the change of gender from πόλεις to αὐτοῖς explains itself): and moreover the tone of rebuke in which this Epistle is couched has rendered its salutation in various respects exceptional.

But when we come to Romans, the term Ecclesia disappears from the salutation, and the designation

H. E. 8

of it by reference to its individual members, which in
1 Corinthians we found combined with Ecclesia, now
stands alone, "to all that are in Rome beloved of
God, called to be saints," each word "beloved[1]" and
"saints[2]" expressing a privilege once confined to
Israel but now extended to the Gentiles. It is the
same in Philippians ("to all the saints in Christ
Jesus that are in Philippi"); and "Ephesians" ("to
the saints that are ⟦in Ephesus⟧ and faithful in
Christ Jesus"); and finally Colossians ("to the saints
and faithful brethren, or holy and faithful brethren,
in Christ that are at Colossae").

This later usage of St Paul is followed by St Peter
(ἐκλεκτοῖς παρεπιδήμοις διασπορᾶς followed after a
few words by ἐν ἁγιασμῷ πνεύματος), and by St Jude
(τοῖς ἐν θεῷ πατρὶ ἠγαπημένοις, καὶ Ἰησοῦ Χριστῷ
τετηρημένοις κλητοῖς).

Connected with this carefulness to keep individual
membership in sight, is the total absence of territorial
language (so to speak) in the designations of local
Ecclesiae. Three times the Ecclesia meant is designated by the adjectival local name of its members,
viz. in the salutations to 1 and 2 Thessalonians (τῇ
ἐκκλησίᾳ Θεσσαλονικέων, "of Thessalonians": this personal description being in effect a partial substitute
for the absence of anything like κλητοῖς ἁγίοις), and

---

[1] See Rom. xi. 28 in connexion with Deut. xxxiii. 12 and other parts
of the Old Testament.   [2] See p. 110.

in a reference to the Ecclesia "of the Laodicenes" (τῇ Λαοδικέων ἐκκλησίᾳ) in Col. iv. 16. In all other cases of a single city the Ecclesia is designated as "*in*" that city: so the salutations of 1 and 2 Corinthians, Romans, Philippians, Ephesians, Colossians; also Cenchreae (Rom. xvi. 1), and each of the seven Ecclesiae of the Apocalypse. When the reference is to a whole region including a number of cities and therefore of Ecclesiae the usage is, on the surface, not quite constant. Twice "in" is used, for Judæa (1 Thess. ii. 14), and Asia (Apoc. i. 4): while in each case the form used can be readily accounted for by the accompanying words which rendered the use of "*in*" the only natural mode of designation, τῶν ἐκκλησιῶν τοῦ θεοῦ τῶν οὐσῶν ἐν τῇ ᾽Ιουδαίᾳ ἐν Χριστῷ ᾽Ιησοῦ, and ταῖς ἑπτὰ ἐκκλησίαις ταῖς ἐν τῇ ᾽Ασίᾳ. In all the other (six) cases, however, these plural designations of a plurality of Ecclesiae are designated by a genitive of the region; the Ecclesiae of Judæa, Gal. i. 22; of Asia, 1 Cor. xvi. 19; of Galatia, 1 Cor. xvi. 1 and the salutation to the Galatians; of Macedonia, 2 Cor. viii. 1; of the nations or Gentiles generally (τῶν ἐθνῶν), Rom. xvi. 4. In these collective instances the simple and convenient genitive could lead to no misunderstanding. But we find no instance of such a form as "the Ecclesia of Ephesus" (a city) or "the Ecclesia of Galatia" (a region). No circumstances had yet arisen which could give propriety to such a form of speech.

It may be well now for the sake of clearness, to reckon up separately, without detail, the various classes of Christian societies to which the term Ecclesia is applied in the Epistles and Apocalypse.

1. (sing. with art.). The original Ecclesia of Jerusalem or Judæa, at a time when there was no other:—Gal. i. 13 ; 1 Cor. xv. 9; Phil. iii. 6 : the occasion of reference in all three cases being St Paul's own action as a persecutor.

2. (sing. with art.). The single local Ecclesia of a city which is named :—Thessalonica (1 Thess. i. 1 ; 2 Thess. i. 1); Corinth (1 Cor. i. 2 ; 2 Cor. i. 1); Cenchreae (Rom. xvi. 1); Laodicea in Asia Minor (Col. iv. 16) ; each of the seven Ecclesiae of Proconsular Asia in Apoc. ii. iii.

3. ἡ ἐκκλησία (sing. and with art.), referring to the individual Ecclesia addressed ; or in one case the Ecclesia of the city from which the Epistle was written :—1 Cor. vi. 4 ; xiv. 5, 12, 23 ; Rom. xvi. 23; 1 Tim. v. 16 ; James v. 14 ; 3 John 9, 10.

4. ἐκκλησία (sing. no art.), referring to any individual Ecclesia :—1 Cor. xiv. 4 ;. 1 Tim. iii. 5, 15 ; and similarly ἐν πάσῃ ἐκκλησίᾳ 1 Cor. iv. 17 ; οὐδεμία ἐκκλησία, Phil. iv. 15.

5. (plur.). The sum of individual Ecclesiae in a named region: Judæa (1 Thess. ii. 14 ; Gal. i. 22); Galatia (1 Cor. xvi. 1 ; Gal. i. 2) ; Macedonia (2 Cor. viii. 1); Asia (Proconsular) 1 Cor. xvi. 19 ; Apoc. i. 4 (and practically vv. 11, 20 *bis*) ; or without a

name, but apparently limited to a region named or
implied in the context. Macedonia (2 Cor. viii. 19)
and Proconsular Asia (Apoc. end of each epistle,
ii. 23 (though with πᾶσαι), and xxii. 16).
6. (plur.). Not of a definite region, nor yet the
sum of all individual Ecclesiae ; 2 Cor. xi. 8 (ἄλλας
ἐκκλησίας) ; viii. 23 (ἀπόστολοι ἐκκλησιῶν) ; and
more collectively πᾶσαι αἱ ἐκκλησίαι τῶν ἐθνῶν of
Rom. xvi. 4, and αἱ ἐκκλησίαι πᾶσαι τοῦ χριστοῦ
of Rom. xvi. 16, which we have seen probably refer
to the Judæan Ecclesiae.
7. (plur.). The sum of all individual Ecclesiae
(or all but the one written to) ; usually with πᾶσαι
(1 Cor. vii. 17, xiv. 33 [with τῶν ἁγίων added] ; 2 Cor.
viii. 18, 24 ; xi. 28) ; with λοιπαί (2 Cor. xii. 13) ; or
simply with τοῦ θεοῦ (2 Thess. i. 4 ; 1 Cor. xi. 16).
8. (sing.). The one universal Ecclesia as represented in the local individual Ecclesia (as in the
address to the Ephesian elders). This is confined
to 1 Cor. (x. 32 ; xi. 22 ; and probably xii. 28).
9. (sing.). The one universal Ecclesia absolutely.
This is confined to the twin Epistles to Ephesians
and Colossians (Eph. i. 22 ; iii. 10, 21 ; v. 23, 24, 25,
27, 29, 32 ; Col. i. 18, 24).
10. (sing.). What may be called a domestic
Ecclesia. This is a subject on which more will probably be known hereafter than at present. Thus far
it seems pretty clear that St Paul's language points
to a practice by which wealthy or otherwise im-

portant persons who had become Christians, among
their other services to their brother Christians, allowed
the large hall or saloon often attached to (or included
in) the larger sort of private houses, to be used as
places of meeting, whether for worship or for other
affairs of the community. Accordingly the Ecclesia
in the house of this or that man, would seem to mean
that particular assemblage of Christians, out of the
Christians of the whole city, which was accustomed
to meet under his roof. The instances are these,
Aquila and Priscilla at Ephesus (1 Cor. xvi. 19); the
same pair afterwards at Rome (Rom. xvi. 5); Nym-
pha (or some would say Nymphas) at Colossae
(Col. iv. 15); and Philemon also at Colossae (Philem.
2).

11. An assembly of an Ecclesia, rather than the
ἐκκλησία itself. This use is at once classical and
a return to the original force of qāhāl. To it belongs
the ἐν ταῖς ἐκκλησίαις of 1 Cor. xiv. 34 (Let the
women be silent in the Ecclesiae); as also, the semi-
adverbial phrases when ἐκκλησία in the singular without an article is preceded by a preposition (ἐν ἐκκλησίᾳ 1 Cor. xi. 18; xiv. 19, 28; ἐνώπιον ἐκκλησίας
3 John 6; analogous to the ἐν συναγωγῇ of John
vi. 59; xviii. 20).

The many Ecclesiae and the one.

In many of the passages here cited, as also in
many passages of the Acts, we have had brought dis-

tinctly before us the individuality of the several local
Ecclesiae in the various cities. On the other hand, apart
from those passages which speak of the one universal
Ecclesia, whether absolutely, or as its attributes are
reflected in a particular Ecclesia, we have varied
evidence as to the pains taken by St Paul to counteract any tendency towards isolation and wantonness
of independence, which might arise in the young
communities which he founded, or with which he
came in contact. The Epistle which contains most
evidence of this kind is 1 Corinthians, the same Epistle
which more than any other is occupied with resisting
tendencies towards inward division. The spirit of
lawlessness would evidently have a disintegrating
effect in both spheres alike, as between the members
of the individual Ecclesia, and as between it and
the sister Ecclesiae of the same or other lands. The
keynote as against isolation is struck in the very
salutation (i. 2). Without going into all the ambi-
guities of language in that verse, we can at least see
that in some manner the Corinthians are there taught
to look on themselves as united to "all who in every
place invoke the name of our Lord Jesus Christ"; and
I believe we may safely add that "theirs and ours"
means "their Lord and ours," the one Lord being set
forth as the common bond of union, and obedience
to His will as Lord, the uniting law of life. Then
in *v.* 9, after giving thanks for those gifts of theirs
which they were in danger of allowing to lead them

astray, he assures them "Faithful is the God through whom ye were called into fellowship of His Son Jesus Christ our Lord,"—fellowship *of* Him, not only fellowship *with* Him, though that also, but fellowship one with another and with all saints, derived from that fellowship with Himself which was common to them all.

Having put before the Corinthians this fundamental teaching at the beginning of the Epistle, St Paul repeatedly afterwards gives it a practical application by his appeals to Christian usage elsewhere. The authorities to which he appeals are of various kinds, e.g. traditions which he had himself first received and then passed on to them and to others, his own personal qualifications for judgment, expediency or edification, the teaching of "nature": but in addition to these he condemns Corinthian practices or tendencies by reference to the adverse practice of other Ecclesiae. Of the praying of women unveiled he says (xi. 16) "We have no such custom, neither the Ecclesiae of God." Enjoining order in the prophesyings (or according to another punctuation the silence of women in the assemblies), he adds (xiv. 33) "as in all the Ecclesiae of the Saints," and with reference to the latter point asks indignantly (*v.* 36) "Is it from you that the word of God came forth, or is it unto you alone that it reached?" In a different and calmer tone he simply seeks a precedent for what he would

have the Corinthians do in the matter of the collection for Judæa (xvi. 1); "as I directed for the
Ecclesiae of Galatia, so do ye also." For a much
larger matter of practice and principle, the remaining
of each convert in the relation of life in which he
previously found himself, he urges (vii. 17) "and so
I direct in all the Ecclesiae"; while in an earlier
passage, he binds up this principle of community with
the obligations created by his personal relation as a
founder (iv. 14—17), bidding them be imitators of
him, as their true father in respect of their new life,
and telling them that he sends them in Timothy
another beloved child of his, "who shall put you in
mind of my ways that are in Christ Jesus, as I teach
everywhere in every Ecclesia."

In other places we find the community between
Ecclesiae brought out from a different point of view
by St Paul's warm thanksgivings for the *going forth*
of the faith and love of this or that Ecclesia towards
other Ecclesiae, so as to be known and to bear fruit
far beyond its own limits (1 Thess. i. 7 f.; iv. 9 f.;
2 Thess. i. 3 f.; 2 Cor. iii. 2; Rom. i. 8; Col. i. 4).
I need not repeat the details of the special prominence given by St Paul to the "collection for the
Saints" as a means of knitting the Gentile and
Jewish Christians together. One practical result of
friendly intercommunion between separate Ecclesiae
would be the cultivation of hospitality, the assurance

that Christians who had need to travel would find a
temporary home and welcome wherever other Christians were gathered together (cf. Rom. xii. 13; 1 Pet.
iv. 9; Heb. xiii. 2; 3 John 5–8). Again, St Paul had
doubtless a deliberate purpose when he rejoiced to
convey the mutual salutations of Ecclesiae (1 Cor. xvi.
19; Rom. xvi. 4, 16; Phil. iv. 22); himself commended
Phoebe to the Romans as one who ministered to the
sister Ecclesia at Cenchreae (Rom. xvi. 1, 2); gave
orders for the exchange of epistles of his, addressed
to two neighbouring Ecclesiae (Col. iv. 16); and made
this or that Ecclesia a sharer, so to speak, in his own
work of founding or visiting other Ecclesiae by allusions to his being *forwarded* by them (προπεμ-
φθῆναι: 1 Cor. xvi. 6; 2 Cor. i. 16; Rom. xv. 24). By
itself each of these details may seem trivial enough:
but together they help to shew how St Paul's recognition of the individual responsibility and sub-
stantial independence of single city Ecclesiae was
brought into harmony with his sense of the unity
of the body of Christ as a whole, by this watchful
care to seize every opportunity of kindling and keeping alive in each society a consciousness of its share
in the life of the great Ecclesia of God.

LECTURE VIII.

THE EARLIER EPISTLES OF ST PAUL.

WE must now pass to the Epistles themselves, taken mainly in chronological order, without however attempting to notice more than a very few of the most instructive passages bearing on our subject. Strictly speaking a large part of them all has a bearing on it, as we must see when once we recognise that in the Apostle's eyes all true life in an Ecclesia is a life of community, of the harmonious and mutually helpful action of different elements, so that he is giving instruction on the very essence of membership when in each of the nine Epistles addressed to Ecclesiae he makes the *peace* of God to be the supreme standard for them to aim at, and the perpetual self-surrender of love the comprehensive means of attaining it.

The Epistles to the Thessalonians.

To begin with 1 Thessalonians. At the outset St Paul dwells much on the marks of God's special love (i. 4), His special choice or election of them (doubtless chiefly at least their election as a com-

munity), as attested in the warmth with which under
severe trials they had embraced the Gospel, and
become imitators of himself and his associates and of
the Lord; so that from them the word of the Lord
had sounded forth anew far and wide. This was
how they came to be an Ecclesia.

Of the temper and attitude which should always
govern the members of an Ecclesia towards each
other preeminently and then further towards all
men, he has much to say in various places, the
foundation being 'love' in accordance with the Lord's
own new commandment, and the comprehensive result, His gift of peace[1]: where, as in iv. 9, φιλαδελφία
comes in, it connotes the special principle of action as
between Christian and Christian, not 'brotherly love',
as A.V. usually has it, i.e. love *like* that of brethren,
but actual 'love of brethren' as being brethren.

Two closely related passages, one in each Epistle,
deserve attention.

In 2 Thess. iii. 6—16 is a remarkable warning
against some brethren among the Thessalonians who
walked 'in an irregular and disorderly way' (ἀτάκτως,
the word carrying with it the association of the verb
ἀτακτέω applied to soldiers who leave their ranks
or who do not keep in rank): they walked, he says,
"not according to the tradition which ye received from
us." The special point would seem to be that on

[1] See 1 Thess. iii. 12; iv. 9—11, &c.

some plea or other, whether of sanctity or gifts of
teaching or the like (we are not told which) they
claimed a specially privileged position, particularly
the privilege of being supported by others. Against
this pretension St Paul sets his own deliberate practice
when among them, how he followed no irregular and
exceptional ways (οὐκ ἠτακτήσαμεν ἐν ὑμῖν), but in
spite of the right which he might have acted on,
worked for his own bread, that he might shew in his
own person an example for all to copy, as well as
not to burden any of them. "And if any," he adds,
"hearkeneth not to our word through the epistle, note
that man not to company with him, that he may be
ashamed (ἐντραπῇ); and count him not as an enemy,
but admonish him as a brother. And may the Lord
of peace Himself give you His peace at all times in
every way." Here we have the beginning of the "discipline" of an Ecclesia, exercised by the community
itself. Seclusion from the society of its members
is seen illustrating by contrast what membership of
an Ecclesia means on its practical side.

The other passage is in 1 Thess. v. 11—15, 23.
Here the practised life of membership is the starting
point. "Wherefore encourage ye one another (παρα-
καλεῖτε ἀλλήλους), and build ye up each[1] the other

---

[1] The Greek here (εἰς τὸν ἕνα) is remarkable, and may be illustrated
by 1 Cor. iv. 6 ἵνα μὴ εἷς ὑπὲρ τοῦ ἑνὸς φυσιοῦσθε κατὰ τοῦ ἑτέρου,
St Paul's point *there* being the dividing effect of inflatedness or puffing
up, as *here* the uniting effect of mutual building up.

as also ye do." Then come two verses in which
St Paul interrupts his words to and about the
Thessalonian Christians generally, in order to call
their attention to a special class among them:
" But we ask you, brethren, to keep in knowledge
(εἰδέναι) them that labour among you and guide
you in the Lord (προϊσταμένους ὑμῶν ἐν Κυρίῳ) and
admonish you, and to esteem them very exceedingly (as we should say 'in a special way' ὑπερεκ-
περισσοῦ or -ῶς) because of their work. Be at peace
in (or among) yourselves." Though it is morally
impossible that προϊσταμένους[1] can here be the technical title of an office standing as it does between
"labouring" and "admonishing", yet the persons meant
are to all appearance office-bearers of the Ecclesia.
The reference is the more interesting because elsewhere in St Paul's Epistles (Pastoral Epistles and
the salutation in Phil. i. 1 excepted) we find no other
mention of such persons as actually existing in any
individual church. It can hardly be doubted that
Elders are meant, though no title is given. The
characteristics assigned to them are three. Their
labouring (κοπιῶντας) is doubtless specially meant
to be opposed to the conduct of such persons as we
have seen denounced in the Second Epistle (iii. 11).
Then comes their guidance, προϊσταμένους, a word

---

[1] This common assumption is further negatived by the prevailing
usage of προΐσταμαι (especially in the present) both in ordinary Greek
and in the New Testament.

usually applied to informal[1] leaderships and managings of all kinds, rather than to definite offices, and associated with the services rendered to dependents by a patron[2], so that (as in Romans) helpful leadership in Divine things would be approximately the thought suggested. Third comes their work of admonition or warning. Of any other form of teaching nothing is said; and probably all three descriptions should be taken as setting forth services rendered to the individual members of the Ecclesia, rather than to the Ecclesia as a whole. After this digression St Paul takes up (1 Thess. v. 14) the thread dropped after *v.* 11 : "But we exhort you, brethren, admonish the disorderly (ἀτάκτους again), encourage the fainthearted, sustain the weak, be longsuffering towards all." The services then which have just been mentioned as specially rendered by the Elders, were not essentially different from services which members of the Ecclesia, simply as brethren, were to render each other. *They* too were to admonish the disorderly, as also to do the converse work of encouraging the feebleminded. *They* too were to make the cause of the weak[3] their own, to sustain them, which is at least one side, if not more,

---

[1] Cf. Rom. xii. 8 ὁ προϊστάμενος ἐν σπουδῇ between two very different clauses.

[2] Cf. Rom. xvi. 2 καὶ γὰρ αὐτὴ (Phoebe) προστάτις πολλῶν ἐγενήθη καὶ ἐμοῦ αὐτοῦ. See p. 207.

[3] Cf. Chrysostom on Rom. xii. 6; Acts xx. 35 (addressed to the Ephesian Elders οὕτως κοπιῶντας δεῖ ἀντιλαμβάνεσθαι τῶν ἀσθενούντων).

of the 'helpful leadership' of the Elders; as well as
to shew long suffering towards all. And again towards the close it is "the God of peace Himself"
that St Paul prays may hallow and keep the Thessalonians.

The Epistles to the Corinthians.

The next Epistle, 1 Corinthians, is perhaps the
richest of all in illustrative matter: but we must
pass through it very quickly. Of late years it has
been the occasion of an interesting theory. Many
people seem to find a difficulty in believing that the
Ecclesiae founded by St Paul in the west, or perhaps
even further east among heathen populations, were
founded on a Jewish basis, such as the Acts seems
to imply, in at least the earlier cases. It has been
pointed out that evidence is fast accumulating (chiefly
from inscriptions) respecting the existence of multitudes of clubs or associations, religious or other, in
the Greek cities of the Empire; and it has been
suggested that in such places as Corinth, the Christian congregation or society was an adaptation rather
of some such Greek models as these than of any Jewish
congregation or society. The presence of these heathen
brotherhoods in the same cities with the new Christian brotherhoods is in any case a striking fact; and
it may be that hereafter traces of their influence may
be detected in the Epistles. But I must confess that
at present, as far as I can see, it is the paucity and

uncertainty of such traces that are chiefly surprising. It would not have been right to pass over so plausible a suggestion in silence: but I fear it will give us no help towards interpreting the evidence of the Epistles themselves.

The first few verses of 1 Corinthians (i. 4—9) after the salutation give us its main theme. St Paul thanks God for the gifts in which these typical Greeks of the Empire were rich, 'speech' and 'knowledge,' and then goes on to warn them against the natural abuse of these gifts, the self-assertion fostered by glibness and knowingness, and the consequent spirit of schism or division, the very contradiction of the idea of an Ecclesia. The habit of seeming to know all about most things, and of being able to talk glibly about most things, would naturally tend to an excess of individuality, and a diminished sense of corporate responsibilities. This fact supplies, under many different forms, the main drift of 1 Corinthians. Never losing his cordial appreciation of the Corinthian endowments, St Paul is practically teaching throughout that a truly Christian life is of necessity the life of membership in a body.

After the thanksgiving he exhorts them (i. 10—17) by the name of our Lord Jesus Christ, the bond of a common service, that they all say the same thing, and there be in them no rents or divisions (σχίσ-ματα), but that they be perfected in the same mind and in the same judgment. He has heard that there

are strifes among them, due to partisanships adorned
with Apostolic names. To all this he opposes the
Cross of the Messiah. Presently (iii. 16 f.) he accounts for all by their forgetfulness that they were a
temple, or shrine of God (for His Spirit by inhabiting
their community or Ecclesia made it into a shrine of
Himself), and he reminds them that this marring of the
temple of God by their going each his own way was
making them guilty of violence against the holiness
of God ; and again further on (iv. 6) he points out
that the party factions which rent the Ecclesia, while
they seemed to be in honour of venerated names, were
in reality only a puffing up of each man against his
neighbour.

With the fifth chapter the concrete practical questions begin. First comes the grievous moral offence
which the Corinthian Christians were so strangely
tolerating in one of their own number. St Paul's
language, circuitous as it may sound, has a distinct
and instructive purpose when closely examined.
The condemnation that he pronounces is not from
a distance or in his own name merely : twice over
he represents himself as present, present in spirit,
in an assembly where the Corinthians and his spirit
are gathered together with the power of our Lord
Jesus. That is, while he is peremptory that the in-
cestuous person shall be excluded from the community,
he is equally determined that the act shall be their
own act, not a mere compliance with a command

of his: "do not ye judge them that are within," he asks, "while them that are without God judgeth? Put away (Deut. xxii. 24) the evil man out of yourselves."

How little this zeal for the purity of the community involved a pitiless disregard of the individual offender we may see from 2 Cor. ii.

The next chapter (vi.) contains a rebuke at once of the litigious spirit which contradicted the idea of a community, and of the consequent habit of having recourse to heathen tribunals rather than the arbitration of brethren.

The eighth chapter lays down the social rule that a man is bound not by his own conscience only, but by the injury which he may do to the conscience of his brethren.

The next three chapters (ix.—xi.) set forth in various ways the entrance into the one body by baptism, and the sustenance of the higher life by that Supper of the Lord[1] in which the mutual communion

[1] In x. 16—21, in arguing against complicity with idolatry through offered meats, he appeals to the one bread which is broken as a Communion of the body of the Christ, and then explains why: "because" he says, "we the many are one bread, one body, for we partake all of us [of bread] from the one bread."

The Holy Communion is more directly the subject of xi. 17—34, the special occasion being the injuries done to Christian fellowship by the practices which were tolerated at the Communion feast still identical with the Agape.

To these differences he applies the same term σχίσματα (v. 18) which in the first chapter he had applied to the parties glorying in Apostolic names.

of members of the body, and the communion of each and all with the Head of the body are indissolubly united.

For our purpose the central chapter is the twelfth, starting from the differences of gifts and proceeding to the full exposition of the relation of body and members. But to this we shall have to return presently, as also to the closing verses setting forth the variety of functions appointed by God in the Ecclesia. Then comes the familiar thirteenth chapter on love, which in the light of St Paul's idea of the Ecclesia we can see to be no digression, this gift of the Spirit being incomparably more essential to its life than any of the gifts which caught men's attention.

Yet these too had their value subordinate as it was, and so in ch. xiv. St Paul teaches the Corinthians what standard to apply to them one with another, these standards being chiefly rational intelligibility, edification, i.e. the good of the community, and fitness for appealing to the conscience of heathen spectators.

2 Cor. contains little fresh but the peculiar verse, ix. 13. The concluding section (xii. 19—xiii. 13) implies the same fears as to breaches of unity as the first Epistle; and it is worth notice from this point of view that in the final benediction the love of God and the communion of the Holy Spirit is added to the usual grace of the Lord Jesus Christ.

Galatians likewise calls now for no special remark.

The Epistle to the Romans.

St Paul's peculiar position towards the Romans invests his Epistle to them with an interest of its own. We saw before that the Ecclesia of Antioch was founded by no Apostle, and, as the Epistle shews, it is the same with that of the mighty Rome, which had sprung up no one knows how, no one knows when, from some promiscuous scattering of the seed of truth ; though a later age invented a founding of both by St Peter. The contrast in St Paul's tone, its total absence of any claim to authority, illustrates how large a part of the authority which he exercised towards other Ecclesiae was not official, so to speak, but personal, involved in his unique position as their founder, their father in the new birth. Here (i. 11 f.) telling the Romans that he longs to see them that he may impart to them some spiritual gift that they may be stablished, he instantly explains himself, " that is that *I with you*[1] may be comforted in you, each of us by the other's faith, both yours and mine."

Almost the whole Epistle is governed by the thought which was filling St Paul's mind at this time, the relation of Jew and Gentile, the place of both in the counsels of God, and the peaceful inclusion of both in the same brotherhood. On the one hand the failure and the obsoleteness of the Law in its letter is set forth more explicitly than ever ; on the

---

[1] Cf. xv. 32 "and *together with you* find rest."

other the continuous growth of the new Ecclesia out
of the old Ecclesia is expounded by the image of
the grafting of the wild Gentile olive into the ancient
olive tree of Israel.

The apparently ethical teaching of chapters xii.
and xiii. is really for the most part on the principles
of Christian fellowship, and rests on teaching about
the body and its members, and about diversity of
gifts resembling what occurs in 1 Corinthians, and
will similarly need further examination presently.

Again ch. xiv. may be taken with 1 Cor. x.

Lastly, the fifteenth and parts of the sixteenth
chapter illustrate historically, as other chapters had
done doctrinally[1], St Paul's yearnings for the unity of
all Christians of East and West, and its association in
his mind with his carrying the Gentile offering to
Jerusalem, and, if he should then escape death, with
his own presence at Rome, the centre and symbol of
civil unity.

---

[1] Note how here also the application of the principle of fidelity to
Christian fellowship in xv. 7 to "mutual reception" ($\pi\rho o\sigma\lambda\alpha\mu\beta\acute{a}\nu\epsilon\sigma\theta\epsilon$
$\dot{a}\lambda\lambda\acute{\eta}\lambda o\nu s$, cf. xiv. 1, 3; xi. 15) is specially connected with the relations
of Jewish to Gentile Christians ; and how once more the same principle
is illustrated from another side by the remarkable section xvi. 17—20
which St Paul interposes as by an afterthought before the original final
salutation, with its warnings against the (unnamed) Judaizers from whom
he feared the introduction of divisions ($\delta\iota\chi o\sigma\tau a\sigma\acute{\iota}as$) and stumblingblocks,
and its confident hope that nevertheless the God of peace would shortly
bruise Satan under their feet, Satan the author of all discord and cunning
calumny, of all that is most opposed to the purposes for which the
Ecclesia of God and His Christ had been founded.

LECTURE IX.

THE ONE UNIVERSAL ECCLESIA IN THE EPISTLES OF THE FIRST ROMAN CAPTIVITY.

WE now enter on that period of the Apostolic Age which begins with St Paul's arrival at Rome. His long-cherished hope was at last fulfilled, though not in the way which he had proposed to himself. He had met face to face the Christian community which had grown up independently of all authoritative guidance in the distant capital ; and, on the way, the Gentile offering which he carried to the Christians of Jerusalem had been accepted by their leaders, and he had escaped, though barely escaped, martyrdom at the hands of his unbelieving countrymen. Delivered from this danger, and shut up for two years at Caesarea, probably with great advantage to the cause for which he laboured, he had reached Rome at last as the prisoner of the Roman authorities. Here he spent another period of two years in another enforced seclusion, which still more evidently gave him a place of vantage for spreading the Gospel such as he could hardly have had as a mere visitor (see Lightfoot, *Phil.* 18 f.). The four extant Epistles belonging to this period are pervaded by a serenity and a sense of assurance such as are rarely to be found in their six predecessors, even in Romans, and this increased happiness of tone is closely connected with St Paul's thoughts and hopes about the various Ecclesiae and about the Ecclesia.

The Epistle to the Philippians.

We begin with the Epistle to the Philippians. The last words of the opening salutation (i. 1) σὺν ἐπισκό-ποις καὶ διακόνοις, "with the bishops (or overseers) and deacons" (R.V.), will be examined to better effect after we have considered the usage of the same words in the Pastoral Epistles.

The special joy which fills the Apostle's mind in his outpourings to the Philippian Christians is called forth by their warm and active fellowship or communion with him, not simply as the messenger of truth to themselves at a former time, but as now and in the future the chief herald of the Gospel to other regions[1]. Their sympathies and aspirations were not shut up within their own little community.

St Paul has likewise much to say to the Philippians on the inward relations of the Ecclesia, for this is the purport of his varied and strenuous exhortations to

---

[1] See i. 5—7 ; 12—20; 25 f.; ii. 17—30; iv. 3, 10, 14—19.

unity, and that on the basis of a corporate life *worthy of the Gospel of Christ.* Such is doubtless the force of the pregnant phrase in i. 27 [R. V. Mg.] 'behave as citizens worthily of the Gospel of the Christ' (μόνον ἀξίως τοῦ εὐαγγελίου τοῦ χριστοῦ πολιτεύεσθε), πολιτεύομαι retaining its strict sense[1] 'to live the life of citizens', not merely the weaker late sense [R. V. text] 'to behave, conduct themselves'. It is thus closely connected with the familiar 'citizenship' (πολίτευμα) of iii. 20, the new commonwealth having its centre in Heaven, to which Christians belong, being implicitly contrasted with the terrestrial commonwealth centred at Jerusalem, resting on laws about mere externals such as circumcision and distinctions of meats. And the same contrast underlies this exhortation to live a community life (πολιτεύεσθε) worthy of the Gospel of the Christ, one directed not by submission to statutes but by the inward powers of the spirit of fellowship ; as St Paul himself explains within the same sentence, "that ye stand fast in one spirit, with one soul wrestling together through the faith of the Gospel" (the faith which it teaches and inspires); and more fully still in the following section (ii. 1—11).

---

[1] This strict sense is similarly the right one, in the only other place of the New Testament where the verb occurs, Acts xxiii. 1, St Paul there using it of himself as one who had loyally lived the life of a true Jew. Various places in some books of the Apocrypha, in Josephus, and nearly a century later in Justin's dialogue with the Jew Trypho, shew that it must have been commonly used by the Jews in this familiar sense.

The Epistle to the 'Ephesians.'

We now come to the three Epistles which the same messenger carried into Asia Minor, the Epistles to the 'Ephesians', to the Colossians, and to Philemon.

The Epistle to Philemon concerns us only by the speaking testimony which it bears to the reality of the Ecclesia as a brotherhood as shown in the new footing on which it was possible for master and slave to stand towards each other without any interference with the status and legal conditions of servitude.

Nor will it be worth our while to give time separately to the Epistle to the Colossians, nearly all that it contains directly pertinent to our subject being contained likewise in 'Ephesians'.

On the other hand 'Ephesians' is peculiarly rich in instructive materials and would repay a much more complete examination than could be attempted within our limits[1]. He would be a bold man who should suppose himself to have fully mastered even the outlines of its teaching: but even the slightest patient study of it must be fruitful, provided we are willing to find in it something more than we have brought to it. On the other hand it is only too easy to exaggerate its exceptional character. Its teaching is, so to speak, the culmination of St Paul's previous teaching, not a wholly new message divided by a sharp line from what had been spoken before. If we enquire into the cause of this culmination, it is not enough to try to

---

[1] See further in Hort's *Prolegomena to Romans and Ephesians.*

account for it solely by mental progress in St Paul, by ampler experience and riper thought. Such progress, wrought by such causes of progress, must of course have existed in the case of a man in whom the free flow of inward life was so little hampered by languor or obstruction ; and, if so, it would naturally reflect itself in his writings. But we have also to remember the significant hint given us in 1 Cor. ii. that the teaching which he addressed to unripe communities was purposely cut down to be proportional to their spiritual state, and that all the while he was cherishing in his own mind a world of higher thoughts, "a wisdom", he calls it, which could rightly be proclaimed only to maturer recipients ; though here and there, for instance in some passages of Romans, he could not refrain from partially admitting others to these inner thoughts. This being the case, he might well desire to make some Christian communities depositaries of this reserved wisdom before he died, and the Ecclesiae of Ephesus and other cities of that region may have seemed to him to have now reached a sufficiently high stage of discipleship to enable them to receive with advantage what he now wished to say. The primary subjects of this higher teaching may be described as the relation of the Son of God to the constitution of the Universe, and to the course of human history, and in connexion with such themes it was but natural that the Ecclesia of God should find a place.

But there were other reasons why St Paul should think and write about the Ecclesia at this time, reasons arising in part at least out of concrete contemporary history. We have already seen how in the period preceding his two captivities his mind was filled with the antithesis of Jew and Gentile within the Christian fold, and with the steady purpose of averting division by his dangerous last journey to Jerusalem, after which he hoped to crown his missions, as it were, by friendly intercourse with the Christians of Rome. The abiding monument of this aspiration is the Epistle to the Romans, and 'Ephesians' is a corresponding monument of the same thoughts from the side of fulfilment instead of anticipation. It is hardly a paradox to. say that neither of these two great Epistles is really intelligible without the other. To a Jew, or a Christian brought up as a Jew, there could be no such cleavage among mankind as that between the people within the old covenant and the promiscuous nations without it. A Christian who understood his own faith could not but believe that the death on Calvary had filled up the chasm, or (in St Paul's figure) dissolved the middle wall of partition. But all would seem to have been done in vain if the work of God were repudiated by wretched human factiousness, and if Jewish Christians and Gentile Christians renounced and spurned each other. This worst of dangers was now to all appearance averted, and so St Paul could expound to the Gentiles of Asia Minor

the uniting counsel of God without serious misgivings
lest perverse human facts should frustrate the great
Divine purpose.

A phrase or two must suffice to quote from
ii. 11—22, "He is our peace who made the both
(τὰ ἀμφότερα neuter) one"; again, "that He might
found the two in Himself into one new man,
making peace, and might reconcile the both (τοὺς
ἀμφοτέρους masc.) in one body to God through
the Cross." Hitherto the Acts and Epistles have
been setting before us only a number of separate independent little communities each called an Ecclesia:
at least this holds good for Gentile Christendom
from Antioch outwards, and perhaps even for Palestine. Now however the course of events has led the
Apostle to think of all Jewish Christians collectively,
and all Gentile Christians collectively, and of both
these two multitudes of men as now made one in the
strictest sense, "one new man". But this fusion is no
mere negative or destructive process. To take away
the distinction of Jew and Gentile without putting
anything better in its place would have been deadly
retrogression, not progress: fusion takes place because
Jewish and Gentile believers alike are members of a
single new society held together by a yet more solemn
consecration than the old, and that new society is
called "the Ecclesia": in other words for Christians it
is true to say that there is one Ecclesia, as well as to
say that there are many Ecclesiae.

It would seem accordingly that to St Paul, when writing this Epistle, "the Ecclesia" was a kind of symbol or visible expression of that wondrous 'mystery', to use his own word, which had been hidden throughout the ages but was now made manifest, that the Gentiles were fellow-heirs and of the same body, and partakers of the same promises in Christ Jesus through the Gospel, and hence that it was likewise, a symbol or visible expression of the Wisdom, as he calls it, by which God was working out His purpose through diversities of ages and by means which seemed for the time to foil Him. This subject is in some respects more fully expounded in Rom. ix.—xi., but without clear mention of the Ecclesia. It is probably in reference to it that St Paul speaks (iii. 10) of the "manifoldly diverse" (or resourceful πολυποίκιλος) wisdom of God, as being made known to the heavenly powers through the Ecclesia, i.e. through beholding the Ecclesia and considering the light which its very existence threw back on dark places of the world's history in the past. Nay through the Apostle's guarded words we may probably gather that the Ecclesia, with these associations attached to it, was to him likewise a kind of pledge for the complete fulfilment of God's purpose in the dim future. Ideally the Ecclesia was coextensive with humanity: all who shared the manhood which Christ had taken were potentially members of the Ecclesia: its ideals were identical with the ideals of a cleansed and perfected humanity. In ascribing glory to Him who is able to do exceeding abundantly above all that we ask or think according to the power which is inwrought in us, he lets us see (iii. 20 f.) what present facts were inspiring this reaching forward of hope, by adding "in the Ecclesia and in Christ Jesus (the Divine Head of the Ecclesia) unto all the generations of the age of the ages."

But if the securing of the union of Jewish and Gentile Christians on equal terms was one cause of St Paul's distinct recognition of the Ecclesia as *one* at this time, his position at Rome must have been another. Although his language in Romans shews that he had no intention of treating the community at Rome as having no legitimate position till he should give it some sort of Apostolic authorisation, he evidently did naturally feel that his function as Apostle of the Gentiles had a certain incompleteness till he had joined in Christian work and fellowship in the capital of the Gentile world, and brought the Roman community into closer relations of sympathy with other Christian communities through the bond of his own person. Writing now from Rome he could not have divested himself, if he would, of a sense of writing from the centre of earthly human affairs ; all the more, since we know from the narrative in Acts xxii. that he was himself a Roman citizen, and apparently proud to hold this place in the Empire.

Here then he must have been vividly reminded of the already existing unity which comprehended both Jew and Gentile under the bond of subjection to the Emperor at Rome, and similarity and contrast alike would suggest that a truer unity bound together in one society all believers in the Crucified Lord. Some generations were to pass before the Christian Ecclesia and the Roman Empire were to stand out visibly in the eyes of men as rivals and at last as deadly antagonists. But even in the Apostolic age the impressiveness of the Empire might well contribute to the shaping of the thoughts of a St Paul about his scattered fellow-believers.

Besides these two causes for the transition from the usage of applying the term Ecclesia only to an individual local community to this late use of it in the most comprehensive sense, we must not forget the biblical associations with the Ecclesia of Israel which were evidently suggestive of unity, and perhaps a similar mode of speech as regards the Christians of Palestine before the Antiochian Ecclesia had come into existence. But apparently these influences did not affect current usage till changed circumstances pointed to the use of a collective name.

The image of the body.

'Ephesians' contains however other definitions of the Ecclesia which are in like manner led up to by

corresponding language in earlier Epistles. The most
important of these is the image of the body. The
cardinal passages are two, in 1 Cor. xii. and in Rom.
xii.: the interesting but difficult allusion in 1 Cor. x.
16, 17 may be passed over. In 1 Cor. xii. St Paul
deals with the vexed question of spiritual powers,
and counteracts the disposition to treat the more exceptional and abnormal kinds of powers as peculiarly
spiritual, by treating all powers as merely different
modes of manifestation of the same Spirit, and each
power as a gift bestowed on its recipient, with a
view to what is expedient (πρὸς τὸ συμφέρον). From
the Spirit and its manifestations he then descends to
the recipients themselves. The reason, it is implied,
why they have received different powers is because
there are different functions to be discharged answering to these several powers; and the meaning of
this difference of functions is explained by the fact
that together they constitute a body, of which each is
a different member "for (*v.* 13) in one Spirit we were
all baptized into one body, whether Jews or Greeks,
whether bond or free, and were all made to drink of
one Spirit." He points out that in a body the whole
is dependent on the diversity of office of the several
members, and that each member is dependent on the
office of the other members. Then he adds, "But ye
are a body of Christ (σῶμα Χριστοῦ), and members
severally." (The next verses we must come to
presently.) Here evidently it is the Corinthian

community by itself that is called a 'body of Christ': this depends not merely on the absence of an article but on $\dot{\nu}\mu\epsilon\hat{\iota}\varsigma$, which cannot naturally mean "all ye Christians."

In Rom. xii. 3—5 all is briefer, but the ideas are essentially the same. The central verse is, "As in one body we have many members, and all the members have not the same office (action), so we the many are one body in Christ, and severally members one of another." Here the language used is not formally applied to the Roman community in particular: but the context shews that St Paul is still thinking of local communities, and of the principles which should regulate the membership of the Roman community, as of all others.

In 'Ephesians' the image is extended to embrace all Christians, and the change is not improbably connected with the clear setting forth of the relation of the Body to its Head which now first comes before us. In the illustrative or expository part of the passage of 1 Cor. indeed (*v.* 21) the head is mentioned; but only as one of the members, and nothing answers to it in what is said of the body of Christ and *its* members. And again in the rather peculiar language of *v.* 12 ($o\mathring{\upsilon}\tau\omega\varsigma$ $\kappa\alpha\grave{\iota}$ $\grave{o}$ $\chi\rho\iota\sigma\tau\acute{o}\varsigma$) Christ seems to be represented by a natural and instructive variation of the image, as Himself constituting the whole body (in accordance with the Pauline phrase $\grave{\epsilon}\nu$ $X\rho\iota\sigma\tau\hat{\wp}$), without reference positively or negatively to the head. This limitation was the more natural in these two cases because in both the main purpose was rather a practical than a doctrinal one, the repression of vanities and jealousies by vivid insistence on the idea of diversity and interdependence of functions. The comparison of men in society to the members of a body was of course not new. With the Stoics in particular it was much in vogue. What was distinctively Christian was the faith in the One baptizing and life-giving Spirit, the one uniting body of Christ, the one all-working, all-inspiring God.

In 'Ephesians' and Colossians the change comes not so much by an expansion or extension of the thought of each local Ecclesia as a body over a wider sphere as by way of corollary or application, so to speak, of larger and deeper thoughts on the place of the Christ in the universal economy of things, antecedent not only to the Incarnation but to the whole course of the world. According to St Paul, as Christ "is before all things and all things ($\tau\grave{a}$ $\pi\acute{a}\nu\tau a$) in Him consist" (Col. i. 17), so also it was God's purpose in the course of the ages "to sum up all things in Him, the things in the heavens and the things on the earth" ($\dot{a}\nu a\kappa\epsilon\phi a\lambda a\iota\acute{\omega}\sigma a\sigma\theta a\iota$ Eph. i. 10: cf. Col. i. 20). Part of this universal primacy of His ($\pi\rho\omega\tau\epsilon\acute{u}\omega\nu$ Col. i. 18), involved in His exaltation to the right hand of God as the completion of His Resurrection, was (Eph. i. 22 f.) that God "gave Him as Head over all things to the Ecclesia which is His body, the fulfilment of

Him who is fulfilled all things in all"; or as in Col. (i. 18) "Himself is the Head of the body, the Ecclesia." The relation thus set forth under a figure is mutual. The work which Christ came to do on earth was not completed when He passed from the sight of men : He the Head, needed a body of members for its full working out through the ages : part by part He was, as St Paul says, to be fulfilled in the community of His disciples, whose office in the world was the outflow of His own. And on the other hand His disciples had no intelligible unity apart from their ascended Head, who was also to them the present central fountain of life and power.

Here, at last, for the first time in the Acts and Epistles, we have "the Ecclesia" spoken of in the sense of the one universal Ecclesia, and it comes more from the theological than from the historical side ; i.e. less from the actual circumstances of the actual Christian communities than from a development of thoughts respecting the place and office of the Son of God : His Headship was felt to involve the unity of all those who were united to Him. On the other hand it is a serious misunderstanding of these Epistles to suppose, as is sometimes done, that the Ecclesia here spoken of is an Ecclesia wholly in the heavens, not formed of human beings. In the closest connexion with the sentences just read St Paul in both Epistles goes on to dwell on the contrast be- tween the past and the present state of the Gentiles

to whom he was writing (and in Eph. ii. 3, in the
spirit of the early chapters of Romans, he intercalates
a similar contrast as true of Jewish converts like
himself), and describes these Gentiles as now "made
alive with the Christ, and raised with Him, and made
with Him to sit in the heavenly regions in Christ
Jesus";—difficult words enough, but clearly turning on
the spiritual union of men actually on earth with One
called their Head in the heavens. Moreover this
passage of Colossians, by what it says (i. 20) of His
making peace through the blood of His Cross, compared with Eph. ii. 13—18, shews that this new
language about the Ecclesia was really in part
suggested by the new assurance that Jew and Gentile,
those near and those far off, were truly brought
together in the one Christian brotherhood.

Once more the identity of the Ecclesia before
spoken of as 'the body of the Christ' with actual
men upon earth, is implied in Col. i. 24, when St Paul
says, "Now I rejoice in my sufferings for *your* sake"
(i.e. assuredly, for the sake of you Gentiles), and then
goes on "and fill up on my part that which is lacking
of the afflictions of the Christ in my flesh for His
body's sake which is the Ecclesia, *whereof I was made
a minister*, according to the dispensation of God which
was given me to youward" etc.

Husband and Wife.

Again the unity of the Ecclesia finds prominent
expression in various language used by St Paul on
the relation of husband and wife (Eph. v. 22—33). The
conception itself he inherited from the later prophets
of the Old Testament, especially with reference to the
covenant established between Jehovah and His people
at Mount Sinai, e.g. Jer. ii. 2 ; Ez. xvi. 60 ; Is. liv. 5
" Thy Maker is thine husband ; the Lord of hosts is
His name and the Holy One of Israel is thy Re-
deemer ; the God of the whole earth shall He be
called." Language of this kind would easily fit itself
on in due time to the *Ecclesia* of Israel for Greek-
speaking Jews, or the *'ēdhāh* (fem.) for Hebrew-speaking?
Jews: it is involved in the allegorical interpretation
eventually given by Jewish commentators to the Book
of Canticles, but there is no reason to think that this
interpretation was as old as the Apostolic age. St
Paul had already applied the prophetic language or
idea to single local Ecclesiae, that of Corinth (2 Cor.
xi. 2 " I espoused you to one husband to present you
to him a chaste virgin, even to the Christ "), and
implicitly that of Rome (Rom. vii. 4). He had also
in 1 Cor. xi. 3 expressed the relation of husband to
wife by the image of the head, associating it in the
same breath with a Headship of the Christ in relation
to each man or husband, and a Headship of God in
relation to Christ. The lowest of these three headships

was probably suggested by the story of the origin of Eve in Genesis ; and the intermediate Headship was a natural application of the idea of the Christ as the second Adam, the true spiritual Head of the human race and so of each member of it : the word ' κεφαλὴ ' doubtless borrowing for the purpose something of the largeness and variation of sense of the Heb. *rō'sh.*

Now, in Eph. v. these various thoughts are brought together in order to set forth what high duties were by the Divine constitution of the human race involved in the relations of husband and wife. That Headship of the human race which was implied in the Christ's being called the Second Adam carried with it *a fortiori* His Headship of the Ecclesia, that chosen portion of the human race, representative of the whole, which is brought into close relation to Himself, and is the immediate object of His saving and cherishing and purifying love, attested once for all by His willing self-sacrifice. St Paul's primary object in these twelve verses is to expound marriage, not to expound the Ecclesia : but it is no less plain from his manner of writing that the thought of the Ecclesia in its various higher relations was filling his mind at the time, and making him rejoice to have this opportunity of pouring out something of the truth which seemed to have revealed itself to him. If we are to interpret "mystery" in the difficult 32nd verse, as apparently we ought to do, by St Paul's usage, i.e. take it as a Divine age-long secret only now at last disclosed, he wished to say that the meaning of that primary institution of human society, though proclaimed in dark words at the beginning of history, could not be truly known till its heavenly archetype was revealed, even the relation of Christ and the Ecclesia, which just before has been once more called His body, and individual Christians members of that body. Taking this passage in connexion with the various references to the Ecclesia which have preceded in the Epistle, it may be regarded as morally certain that the Ecclesia here intended is not a local community, but the community of Christians as a whole.

LECTURE X.

'GIFTS' AND 'GRACE.'

HAVING thus examined the chief passages of Ephesians, which now for the first time in St Paul's extant Epistles clearly set forth the conception of a single universal Ecclesia, we must return to the passages of various dates in which he expounds his doctrine of χαρίσματα, and exemplifies it by various functions within the Ecclesia. The three passages are 1 Cor. xii. 4—11 and 28—31 ; Rom. xii. 6—8 ; Eph. iv. 7—12.

The meaning of the terms.

Χάρισμα comes of course from χαρίζομαι; it means anything given of free bounty, not of debt, contract, or right. It is thus obviously used in Philo, and as obviously in Rom. v. 15, vi. 23 (the gift of God is eternal life); and less obviously but with I believe essentially the same force in the other passages of St Paul, as also in the only other New Testament place, 1 Pet. iv. 10. In these instances it is used to designate either what we call 'natural advantages' independent of any human process of acquisition, or advantages freshly received in the course of Providence; both alike being regarded as so many various free gifts from the Lord of men, and as designed by Him to be distinctive qualifications for rendering distinctive services to men or to communities of men. In this sense they are Divine gifts both to the individual men in whom so to speak they are located, and to the society for whose benefit they are ordained. This conception underlies not only the passages of St Paul which refer directly to membership of a body, but the various usages of the remaining passages, in which on a superficial view the word might be supposed to be used arbitrarily. (The usage of the Pastoral Epistles we shall have to examine separately by-and-by.) Thus in Rom. xi. 29 ("The gifts and the calling of God are beyond repentance," He cannot change His purpose in respect of them) we have a saying of the utmost universality respecting God's χαρίσματα in general, the special application being to the various privileges granted to Israel for the benefit of mankind. In 1 Cor. vii. 7 χάρισμα is the proper gift which each man has from God as bearing on marriage or celibacy, probably with reference to what St Paul believed to be involved in his own special χάρισμα as the wandering herald of the truth to the Gentiles. In 2 Cor. i. 11 (cf. *vv.* 3—7, 9, 13 f.) it is his recent deliverance from impending death regarded as a gift bestowed on him for the sake of the Gentiles to whom he had yet to preach. And in the anxiously reserved language of Rom. i. 11 it seems to be some advantage connected with his personal history and work, which he wished to share with the Romans (μεταδῶ) by meeting them face to face, for the strengthening of their faith (cf. 1 Thess. ii. 8).

This conception of χάρισμα is essentially the same as that of the talents in the Parable, if only we go behind the somewhat vulgarised modern associations of the word talents to its full sense in the Gospel; with the difference that the Pauline χαρίσματα, covering the members of a body, have a more distinct reference to variety of use. Perhaps the clearest exposition is St Peter's (1 Pet. iv. 9—11, " Each, as he received a χάρισμα, ministering it to one another as good stewards of a manifold bounty (χάριτος) of God"); the instances given being hospitality and teaching. The single fountain of God's bounty or grace is thus represented as dividing itself manifoldly through all the inequalities of human faculty and possessions, that it may be the better distributed by the individual men as stewards each of what he has received, that it may be for the benefit of the great household.

It is important to notice that the associations connected with the term 'grace' as inherited by us from Latin theology, denoting a spiritual power or influence, whether received by individuals according to their need or appropriated permanently to a sacred ordinance or a sacred office, whatever may be the truth of the idea in itself, are only misleading in the interpretation of the biblical language respecting χάρις and χάρισμα. The dominant conception of χάρις in the Acts and the Epistles is the free bounty of God as exhibited in the admission of the Gentiles although they stood without the original covenant; and this is constantly associated in St Paul's mind with the free bounty of forgiveness shown to himself the persecutor, making him the fittest of all heralds of the free χάρις, so preeminently in his own person a recipient of χάρις. And moreover the language in which he is accustomed to speak of the χάρις shown (in biblical language 'given') to him is by him transferred to those parts or aspects of the χάρις shown to Christians generally which constitute separate χαρίσματα. From this point of view it is well worth while to compare 1 Cor. iii. 10; Gal. i. 15, ii. 9; Rom. i. 5, xii. 3, xv. 15; Eph. iii. 2, 7, 8; and then to notice how in 1 Cor. i. 4—6 St Paul similarly thanks God, "for the *grace* of God which was given you in Christ Jesus; that in everything ye were enriched in him, in all utterance and all knowledge,...so that ye fall short in no χάρισμα": and again how Rom. xii. 6, "having χαρίσματα in accordance with the χάρις that was given (shown) to us, different [χαρίσματα]," looks back to *v.* 3, and how Eph. iv. 7 looks back to iii. 2, 7, 8.

The source of the ' Gifts.'

To come now to the instances given of various χαρίσματα within the Ecclesia, or of the persons to whom such χαρίσματα were assigned, we may look chiefly at 1 Cor. xii. and Eph. iv. First should be noticed the two verbs by which God's relation to the various functions is expressed in the two Epistles severally. In 1 Cor. the leading thought is of the Divinely ordained diversity of members in the Christian body; hence in *v.* 18 " God ἔθετο (not merely 'set' but 'placed,' set as part of a plan) the members, each one of them in the body as He willed "; and so in *v.* 28 the same verb is repeated with obvious reference to the preceding exposition, " And some God placed in the Ecclesia, first apostles, etc." In Ephesians the Divine χάρις or free bounty is the leading thought, each function being pronounced to be a Divine gift. Ps. lxviii. 18, in the form in which it is quoted in *v.* 8, supplies the verb 'gave' ("and gave gifts to men"), and so St Paul proceeds, "And Himself gave some as apostles, and some as prophets, etc." The *word* χάρισμα does not occur in Ephesians: but ἔδωκεν in this connexion, associated with ἡ χάρις, is exactly the ἐχαρίσατο implicitly contained in χάρισμα.

' Functions' not formal ' Offices.'

Then come the functions themselves. Much profitless labour has been spent on trying to force the

various terms used into meaning so many definite
ecclesiastical offices. Not only is the feat impossible,
but the attempt carries us away from St Paul's
purpose, which is to shew how the different functions
are those which God has assigned to the different
members of a single body. In both lists apostles and
prophets come first, two forms of altogether exceptional function, those who were able to bear witness of
Jesus and the Resurrection by the evidence of their
own sight—the Twelve and St Paul—and those whose
monitions or outpourings were regarded as specially
inspired by the Holy Spirit. Each of these held one
kind of function, and next to these in 1 Cor. come all
who in any capacity were "teachers" (διδάσκαλοι)
without any of the extraordinary gifts bestowed on
apostles and prophets. In Ephesians this function is
given in a less simple form. First there are "evangelists," doubtless men like Titus and Timothy (2 Tim.
iv. 5) and Tychicus and Epaphras, disciples of St Paul
who went about from place to place preaching the
Gospel in multiplication and continuation of his
labours without possessing the peculiar title of apostleship. Probably enough in St Paul's long imprison-
ment this kind of work had much increased. Then
come "pastors and teachers," men who taught within
their own community, and whose work was therefore
as that of shepherds taking care for a flock. Here
the list in Ephesians ends, while that in 1 Cor. proceeds to various functions unconnected with teaching

and belonging rather to action, first, extraordinary
powers and what St Paul calls gifts of healings ; then
two types of ordinary services rendered to members
of the community, first helps[1] (ἀντιλήμψεις), anything
that could be done for poor or weak or outcast brethren,
either by rich or powerful or influential brethren or by
the devotion of those who stood on no such eminence ;
and secondly guidances[2] or governments (κυβερνήσεις),
men who by wise counsels did for the community what
the steersman or pilot does for the ship. Then last
comes an exceptional class of extraordinary powers or
manifestations, neither properly didactic nor properly
practical, what are called 'tongues'. The enumeration earlier in the chapter (vv. 8—10) not only omits
apostles and helps and guidances, but, with other
variations, seems to subdivide the function of teachers
under three different qualifications, what are called
"an utterance (λόγος) of wisdom," "an utterance of
knowledge," and "faith": and in Rom. xii. there are
analogous subdivisions, among which occurs "ministration" (διακονία), a very comprehensive word,
including e.g. (1 Cor. xvi. 15) the way in which
apparently the household of Stephanas laid themselves out (ἔταξαν ἑαυτούς) to be hospitable and
helpful to Christian strangers visiting Corinth.

[1] Cf. Acts xx. 35 ἀντιλαμβάνεσθαι τῶν ἀσθενούντων, some places in
LXX., but especially Ecclesiasticus [xi. 12 ; li. 7].

[2] See especially its use in the LXX. version of Proverbs as the
apparently exactly literal rendering of tăkhbūlōth (see Del. on Prov.
i. 5), three times rendered 'wise guidance' in R.V.

All this variation of enumeration, and also the
variation in the form of description (persons and so to
speak things being terms of a single series), becomes
intelligible and natural when we understand clearly
that St Paul is not speaking at all of formal offices or
posts in the Ecclesia, much less enumerating them.
The chief reason why he *seems* to do this is because
apostles stand at the head in the two chief lists, and
the apostolate of the Twelve and St Paul was in an important sense a definite and permanent office. But it
was part of St Paul's purpose to shew that the service
which they were intended to render to the Ecclesia
of that age was on the one hand, as in the other
cases, the service[1] of members to a body to which
they themselves belonged, and on the other was too
peculiar to be included under any other head. What
is common in substance to all the terms of the series
is that they are so many kinds of partial service, and
from this point of view it was immaterial whether
there were or were not definite offices corresponding
to any or all of these kinds of service ; 'or again
whether two or more kinds of service were or were
not, as a matter of fact, ever performed by the same
persons. Hence these passages give us practically no
evidence respecting the formal arrangements of the
Ecclesiae of that age, though they tell us much of the
forms of activity that were at work within them, and

---

[1] Cf. 1 Cor. iii. 5—9, and indeed —15, on Apollos and Paul.

above all illustrate vividly St Paul's conception of an Ecclesia and of the Ecclesia.

The image of the ' Body.'

The passage of Ephesians which we have been examining (iv. 7—11) begins the second portion of a section which rings with the proclamation of the great supreme Christian unities. But the purpose for which they are set forth is to sustain an exhortation on the fundamental practical duty attached to membership of the Christian body, to walk worthily of the vocation wherewith ye were called (explained by Col. iii. 15, "Let the peace of the Christ preside in your hearts, unto which ye were also called in [one] body "—better to read "in a body," i.e. to be members of a body) with all lowliness and meekness etc., giving diligence to keep the unity of the Spirit in the bond of peace : one body and one Spirit, he proceeds in the familiar words which seem to glide from exhortation addressed to Christians of a few cities of Asia into affirmation respecting the whole body of Christians. But it would seem as though he dreaded the very semblance of representing an Ecclesia of God as intended to be a shapeless crowd of like and equal units. Accordingly he turns within, to claim as it were all varieties and inequalities as so many indications of divers functions needed to work together to a true unity. "To each one of us," he says emphatically (Ἑνὶ δὲ ἑκάστῳ ἡμῶν), "was given the grace according to the measure of the

bounty of the Christ." Then comes the quotation
from the Psalm and the rapid setting forth of apostles,
prophets, evangelists, pastors and teachers as so
many various gifts of God to men ; and then in the
same breath their present and their ultimate purposes ;
their present purpose the καταρτισμός, or perfecting
and accomplishing of the saints (i.e. the individual
members of the great community) unto a work of
ministration (i.e. those more conspicuous functions
were meant to train and develop analogous functions
of ministration, in each and all) ; then secondly, as a
single aim of this manifold accomplishing, the building
up of the body of the Christ ; and finally, as the
ultimate purpose of these processes, the attainment of
all together (οἱ πάντες), unto the unity of the faith and
of the knowledge of the Son of God, unto a perfect
[full-grown] man, unto a measure of stature [maturity]
of [such as belongs to] the fulfilment of the Christ.
Even here the sentence does not end. From the lofty
heights of his own thought St Paul descends to its
practical purport, the rising out of the old heathen
state of distracted beguilement by unworthy teachers,
and through a life of truthful intercourse one with
another in the power of love (see 25 ff.) growing up
into Him in all things who is the Head, Christ.
Then he ends with a description of the action so to
speak of the Head on the body of the Ecclesia, the
fitting together and knitting together of the whole,
the spreading of life as from a centre through every

joint by which it is supplied, the action of each part in due measure in appropriating and using the life so supplied, and as the result the growth of the Body unto building up of itself in the power of love.

The image of 'building.'

Twice here the image of the body has been supplemented by the image of building. In various forms this other image is widely spread through the apostolic writings, not only in the simple thought of building up as opposed to the contrary process of pulling down or dissolving and to the simulative process of puffing up; but as exhibiting the ranging of human beings side by side so as to form together a stable structure of various parts, all resting on a foundation. But the ruling element in the idea comes naturally from the special purpose of the building. It is a dwelling-place or house, and its inhabitant is God; so that it is further a sanctuary (ναός) or temple of God. When our Lord Himself said in the temple at Jerusalem, "Destroy (dissolve, λύσατε) this temple and in three days I will raise it up," interpreted by St John to refer to the temple of His body, He must surely have been chiefly thinking of that temple, that body of His which St Paul identifies with the Ecclesia, for from the day of the Passion the temple of stones lay under doom. Such at all events was Stephen's teaching so far as the old temple is concerned, when to the words of 1 Kings viii., how Solomon

built Jehovah a house he added the comment, " How-
beit the Most High dwelleth not in things made with
hands," appealing to Is. lxvi. " Heaven is my throne,"
etc. Such was also the teaching of his persecutor
and disciple St Paul when at Athens he repeated how
the Creator, being Lord of heaven and earth, dwelleth
not in temples made with hands. The positive side
of the same teaching we have in St Paul's adaptation
of Lev. xxvi. in 2 Cor. vi. 16, " For we are a sanctuary
of a living God, as God said, I will dwell in them and
walk in them, and I will be their God, and they shall
be my people," where that second phrase, " and walk in
them" marks the indwelling spoken of to be not of a
carved image or of a vaguely conceived presence but
of a living God.   Here as also in the yet more
familiar passage 1 Cor. iii. 16 f. (" Know ye not that
ye are a sanctuary of God, and the Spirit of God
dwelleth in you?"), the individual local community is
itself addressed as a sanctuary of God ; and the same
conception, if we are not to disregard both grammar
and natural sense, is expressed with great generality
in Eph. ii. 21 f. "in whom [i.e. Christ Jesus as Corner-
stone] each several building (R.V.) ($\pi \hat{a} \sigma a$ $o i \kappa o \delta o \mu \acute{\eta}$)
fitly framed together groweth into a holy temple in
the Lord, in whom ye also are builded together for a
habitation of God in the Spirit."   Indeed, if I mistake
not, the thought of a universal spiritual temple of
God is, to say the least, not definitely expressed
anywhere by St Paul.

The foundation of the Apostles and Prophets.

Before we leave the language derived from a building, one very familiar phrase in Ephesians ii. 20 claims notice, "built upon the foundation of the apostles and prophets," which may be interpreted and has been interpreted in several different ways. To find who are meant by the apostles and prophets we must first take this passage with another (iii. 5 f.), "the mystery of the Christ, which in other generations was not made known to the sons of men as it was now revealed to His holy apostles and prophets in spirit, that the Gentiles are fellow-heirs and of the same body," etc. etc. The position of "prophets" as second in both places puts the Old Testament prophets out of the question, unless indeed they were likewise meant by "the apostles", which in c. iii. is impossible. It seems to me that both the sense of both places and the collocation of words in c. iii. determine the apostles themselves to be the prophets meant. It is truly said that we cannot lay much stress on the absence of a second article before 'prophets'; but in iii. 5 the prefixing of ἁγίοις and subjoining of αὐτοῦ to ἀπο-στόλοις is difficult to account for, if the prophets meant were a second set of persons. Such a passage as Gal. i. 15 [1] is enough to suggest that St Paul regarded the office of the old prophets as in some way repeated in himself; and if we consider such

---

[1] Cf. Is, xlix. 1.

sayings of our Lord on the last evening as John xiv.
26; xv. 26 f.; xvi. 13 ff. on the office of the second
Paraclete in relation to the disciples, we must see
that so far as the words had a first and special
reference to the apostolic band, their witness-bearing
to Christ was conditioned by the interpretative and
enlightening operation of the Holy Spirit, and further
that utterances proceeding from such an operation
exactly answer to what the Bible calls prophecy. In
a word, the specially chosen disciples had need to be
prophets in order to be in the strict sense apostles.
The full revelation respecting the Gentiles to which
St Paul refers in Eph. iii. 6 ff. was not obviously
involved from the first in the charge to preach the
Gospel to all nations. It was to St Paul himself
doubtless that this prophetic illumination came in the
first instance: but he might well rejoice to merge his
own individuality in the concordant acceptance of
what he had proclaimed by the twelve at Jerusalem,
an acceptance which might well itself be referred to
the inspiration of the prophetic spirit. The enumeration in iv. 11, "And Himself gave some to be apostles,
and some prophets" is not a serious difficulty in the
way of this interpretation, for, as we saw before, the
enumeration is not of classes of persons or formal
offices, but of classes of functions; and though in the
true sense there were no apostles but the twelve and
St Paul, we know there were many others who were
called prophets.

But in what sense were the heathen converts of
Asia "built upon the foundation of the apostles and
prophets"? The phrase might mean either the foundation on which the apostles and prophets had been
built, or the foundation laid by them, or themselves as
the foundation. That Christ Himself is here meant
as the foundation, as 1 Cor. iii. 11 might suggest, is
very unlikely, when the next clause makes Him
cornerstone without any indication that there is a
transition from one figure taken from building to
another with reference to the same subject. The
previous verse in 1 Cor. (iii. 10) and the other passage
of Eph. (iii. 5) suggest that the apostles and prophets
were the builders who laid the foundation ; but it
remains difficult to see what foundation they can be
said to have laid, in connexion with which Christ
could be called a cornerstone. It would seem then
that they themselves constituted the foundation in
the sense which the Gospels led us to recognise, the
chosen band of intimate disciples, the first rudi-
mentary Ecclesia, on which the Ecclesia of Palestine
was first built, and then indirectly every other
Ecclesia, whether it had or had not been personally
founded by an apostle. The reason why they are
designated here by this full and double title is
because the reference here is to the building up of
Gentile Ecclesiae, and. because the admission of the
Gentiles on absolutely equal terms was in St Paul's
mind associated with what were to him leading

characteristics of apostleship and of prophecy under
the New Covenant.

The Universal Ecclesia and the partial Ecclesiae.

We have been detained a long time by the importance of the whole teaching of 'Ephesians' on the
Ecclesia, and especially of the idea now first definitely
expressed of the whole Ecclesia as One. Before
leaving this subject, however, it is important to notice
that not a word in the Epistle exhibits the One Ecclesia as made up of many Ecclesiae. To each local
Ecclesia St Paul has ascribed a corresponding unity
of its own ; each is a body of Christ and a sanctuary
of God : but there is no grouping of them into
partial wholes or into one great whole. The members
which make up the One Ecclesia are not communities
but individual men. The One Ecclesia includes all
members of all partial Ecclesiae ; but its relations to
them all are direct, not mediate. It is true that, as
we have seen, St Paul anxiously promoted friendly
intercourse and sympathy between the scattered
Ecclesiae ; but the unity of the universal Ecclesia as
he contemplated it does not belong to this region : it
is a truth of theology and of religion, not a fact of
what we call Ecclesiastical politics. To recognise
this is quite consistent with the fullest appreciation
of aspirations after an external Ecclesiastical unity
which have played so great and beneficial a part in
the inner and outer movements of subsequent ages.

At every turn we are constrained to feel that we can learn to good effect from the apostolic age only by studying its principles and ideals, not by copying its precedents.

I said just now that the one Ecclesia of Ephesians includes all members of all partial Ecclesiae. In other words, there is no indication that St Paul regarded the conditions of membership in the universal Ecclesia as differing from the conditions of membership in the partial local Ecclesiae. Membership of a local Ecclesia was obviously visible and external, and we have no evidence that St Paul regarded membership of the universal Ecclesia as invisible, and exclusively spiritual, and as shared by only a limited number of the members of the external Ecclesiae, those, namely, whom God had chosen out of the great mass and ordained to life, of those whose faith in Christ was a genuine and true faith. What very plausible grounds could be urged for this distinction, was to be seen in later generations : but it seems to me incompatible with any reasonable interpretation of St Paul's words. On the other hand, it is no less clear that this Epistle, which so emphatically expounds the doctrine of the Christian community, is equally emphatic in recognition of the individual life of its members. The universal Ecclesia and the partial Ecclesiae alike were wholly made up of men who had each for himself believed, whose baptism was for each the outward expression of what was involved in his belief, for his past and for his future; and who had a right to look on the fact that they had been permitted to be the subjects of this marvellous change, as evidence that they had each been the object of God's electing love before the foundations of the world were laid.

LECTURE XI.

TITUS AND TIMOTHY IN THE PASTORAL EPISTLES.

LEAVING now the Epistles of the Roman Captivity we come to the Pastoral Epistles. On the questions of their authenticity and integrity I shall say no more now than that in spite of by no means trivial difficulties arising from comparison of the diction of these and the other Epistles bearing St Paul's name, I believe them to be his, and to be his as they now stand. The supposed difficulties of other kinds seem to me of no weight. About St Paul's life after the time briefly noticed in the last verse of Acts, we know absolutely nothing from any other source beyond the bare fact of his death at Rome: and it is to the interval between the Roman Captivity mentioned in Acts and his death that the Epistles, with the recent incidents referred to in them, must assuredly belong. They differ essentially from all his Epistles except Philemon by being addressed to individual men, not to communities ; while they differ

no less from Philemon in having the welfare of
Christian communities as indirectly a large part of
their subject-matter.

The interpretation of I Tim. iii. 14 f.

This is definitely expressed in an important passage
which we may well consider first, as it is the chief
passage in which the term ἐκκλησία occurs, 1 Timothy
iii. 14 f. " These things I write to thee, hoping to come
unto thee shortly ; but if I tarry long, that thou
mayest know how men ought to behave themselves
in a household of God, which is an Ecclesia of a
living God, a pillar and stay of the truth."
The A. V. (and R. V. *marg.*) rendering "how thou
oughtest to behave thyself" is doubtless a survival of
the Vulgate *quomodo te oporteat*, a translation of the
Western σε. But though the special ἀναστροφή of
Timothy is included, the ἀναστροφή of each class
mentioned and of all members of the Ecclesia is
likewise included. 'Αναστροφή, for which there is no
good English equivalent, includes all conduct and
demeanour in converse with other men. Thus St
Paul here describes his purpose in writing so as to
point out what is a well-ordered life for Christian men
in converse with each other. The force of the words
that follow is only weakened and diluted by treating
the absence of articles as immaterial. The close and
obvious relations subsisting within each single Christian community afford the framework, as it were,

for the teaching; and in instructing its members to regard it as invested with these high attributes St Paul was but doing as he had done to other Ecclesiae before.

The 'house of God' here spoken of is doubtless not His dwelling-house or sanctuary but (as several recent commentators) His household[1]. It is the same ten verses back, "If a man knoweth not how to rule his own household, how shall he take care of an Ecclesia of God"? The same sense 'household' occurs also in Heb. iii. 5 f., x. 21 (from Num. xii. 7) and probably in 1 Pet. iv. 17. It is also implied in St Paul's own use of the adjective οἰκεῖος, probably in Gal. vi. 10, "them that are of the household of the faith"; certainly in Ephesians ii. 19, "fellow citizens with the saints, and of the household of God." Hence the ἀναστροφή or converse described as the subject of this part of the Epistle, is the converse of members of a household of which God is the Householder or Master.

Further it is described as "an Ecclesia of a living God." Often the (a) living God is spoken of in contrast to dead idols: but sometimes (e.g. Heb. iii. 12; ix. 14; xii. 22) it implies a contrast with the true God made practically a dead deity by a lifeless and rigid form of religion; with the God in short in whom

---

[1] The word 'house' is not incorrect, but only ambiguous : in Acts xvi. 34 both senses stand together, the jailor at Philippi brings Paul and Silas *into his house*, and rejoices greatly *with all his house*.

too many of the Jews virtually believed. Such is probably the force here as it evidently is in iv. 10.

The last designation here given to a local Christian community is "a pillar and stay of the truth."

There are few passages of the New Testament in which the reckless disregard of the presence or absence of the article has made wilder havoc of the sense than this. To speak of either *an* Ecclesia or *the* Ecclesia, as being *the* pillar of the truth, is to represent the truth as a building, standing in the air supported on a single column. Again there is no clear evidence that the rare word ἑδραίωμα ever means 'ground[1]' = "foundation." It is rather, in accordance with the almost[2] universal Latin rendering *firmamentum*, a "stay" or "bulwark".

St Paul's idea then is that each living society of Christian men is a pillar and stay of "the truth" as an object of belief and a guide of life for mankind, each such Christian society bearing its part in sustaining and supporting the one truth common to all.

But while at least two of the Pastoral Epistles, and in a certain sense all of them, have thus the Ecclesiae for themselves to a great extent as the subject matter, they are still more truly in substance no less than in obvious form, instructions to individual men,

---

[1] Probably translated by Tyndale from Luther's *Grundfeste*.

[2] *Fundamentum* occurs in *Iren. lat.* [III. i. 1 ; but possibly as a translation of στήριγμα, see III. xi. 8. Ed.]

having special responsibilities of leadership or guidance, and, as regards two of the Epistles, entrusted
definitely with the special charge of Ecclesiae, though
only for limited and temporary purposes. The purposes in the two cases were by no means identical,
though they had much in common.

The mission of Titus in Crete.

The case of Titus is the simplest. He had been
a convert from heathenism, made by St Paul himself
(γνησίῳ τέκνῳ, i. 4), we do not know in what region.
St Paul had taken him with him from Antioch to
Jerusalem at the time of the great conference, and
had refused to yield to pressure and let him be circumcised. He had employed him on a confidential
mission to the Corinthian Ecclesia. This is all that
is known of his antecedents: in the Acts he is not
mentioned by name. After a long interval he now
re-emerges into. light, though only somewhat dim
light. During a journey subsequent to the first
Roman Captivity he had accompanied St Paul on a
visit to the island of Crete. There are various indications in the Epistle that the Christian faith must
have gained ground in the island long before this time:
but at what time, and by whose preaching, we know
not. It would seem that St Paul found the state of
things unsatisfactory, but that he had no time to stay
in person to attempt to rectify it. Accordingly he
left Titus behind to correct, he says, the deficiencies

and to appoint Elders in the several cities. Thus Titus was in this respect to do what Paul and Barnabas had done in the cities of Southern Asia Minor on their return from the first Missionary journey. But the circumstances were very different. The natural inference is that up to this time the Christians of Crete had gone on without any kind of responsible government, and that this anarchic condition was one considerable cause of the evidently low moral condition to which they had sunk. Accordingly the appointment of elders was a necessary first step towards raising the standard of Christian life generally. Zenas and Apollos were now starting on a journey in the course of which they were to touch at Crete, and so St Paul takes the opportunity of sending this letter, partly to remind Titus of the chief things to be attended to in this Mission, partly to prepare him for rejoining St Paul with all possible speed at Nicopolis so soon as Artemas or Tychicus should come to him. When 2 Timothy was written, he had gone to Dalmatia (iv. 10). Why Artemas or Tychicus was to be sent to Titus, is not mentioned; but in all probability whichever of them went was intended to take Titus's place, and give the scattered Ecclesiae of the island the benefit of a little longer superintendence till the newly appointed Elders should have gained some really effective influence under the difficult circumstances of their new office.

Timothy's mission in Ephesus.

The immediate occasion of Timothy's mission resembled that of Titus's mission. He too was evidently journeying with St Paul when they came to Ephesus, and the state of things in the Ephesian Ecclesia appeared to call for a longer and more comprehensive treatment than St Paul had himself time to apply, as he was journeying on to Macedonia. Accordingly he left Timothy behind, specially to resist the growth of certain barren and unprofitable teachings which were evidently gaining much ground at Ephesus. He was in hopes (iii. 14) of rejoining Timothy shortly, but in case of possible delay he desired to keep before Timothy's mind the true aims which he should follow in helping to guide the Ephesian Ecclesia into right and salutary ways.

With the second Epistle we have little to do. It is silent about the affairs of an Ecclesia except so far as they are involved in the qualifications of an evangelist and associate of St Paul. Much of the first Epistle is an outpouring of St Paul's thoughts for his cherished disciple, and the second Epistle is almost wholly of this character, with the added force that came from a sense of his own impending martyrdom. We do not even know with any certainty whether Timothy was still at Ephesus, though probably enough he was: that is, the supposition would harmonise with some of the details respecting other persons, though

in other respects the supposed indications are quite
worthless. Wherever Timothy was, St Paul urges his
making a point (σπούδασον) of coming to him quickly
(2 Tim. iv. 9), bringing Mark with him, for he was left
alone. It is probable enough that the sending of
Tychicus to Ephesus mentioned in iv. 12 was intended
to carry on further Timothy's work there: but we
learn no particulars.

Timothy's antecedents.

On the other hand a special interest attaches to
the language used in several places of both Epistles
respecting Timothy himself. Every one will remember how closely he is associated with St Paul's labours
and writings from the time of the 'second missionary
journey' in Asia Minor, so that his name stands with
St Paul, at the head of six of the earlier epistles, and
occurs in two others of them. Behind this confidential intercourse and cooperation, however, there lay
the exceptional circumstances out of which they arose.
These circumstances are but imperfectly known to us,
but something of their significance comes clearly out
in comparison of St Luke's account in the Acts
(xvi. 1—4) and the language of the Pastoral Epistles,
each of which illustrates the other. When Paul and
Barnabas after returning from the Jerusalem Conference had been for some time preaching at Antioch,
St Paul proposed to Barnabas that they should
revisit the brethren in the various cities of Asia Minor

where they had founded Ecclesiae. The dispute
about Barnabas's cousin St Mark made it impossible
to carry out the plan as first intended. Barnabas and
his cousin went off to his native Cyprus. St Paul
chose for his companion Silas, one of the Jerusalem
envoys who had accompanied the returning Antiochian envoys, a man having prophetic gifts; and
"being commended" we read "to the grace of the
Lord by the brethren, he (Luke does not say 'they,' but
'he') passed through Syria and Cilicia confirming the
Ecclesiae. In due time he reached Lycaonia, specially
its cities Derbe and Lystra: "And behold" (says St
Luke, a phrase which when writing in his own person
and sometimes even in speeches he reserves for
sudden and as it were providential interpositions[1]),
"And behold a certain disciple was there, Timothy by
name, son of a Jewish woman that believed and a
Greek father, one who had witness borne to him
(ἐμαρτυρεῖτο) by the brethren that were at Lystra and
Iconium: him St Paul willed to go forth with him
(τοῦτον ἠθέλησεν ὁ Παῦλος σὺν αὐτῷ ἐξελθεῖν) and he
took and circumcised him, because of the Jews that were
in those parts, for all of them (ἅπαντες) knew that his
father was a Greek. And as they (plural) went on
their way through the cities they delivered them the
δόγματα to keep, which had been resolved on (κεκριμένα) by the apostles and elders that were at Jerusalem". This narrative needs but little paraphrase to

---

[1] See i. 10; viii. 27; x. 17; xii. 7.

become transparent, as far as it goes. Timothy's
Greek father like many Greeks and Romans of wealth
or position in those days, had married a Jewish wife.
He allowed his wife to bring up their boy in her own
faith, but not to brand him with what to Greek eyes
was the infamous brand of circumcision. As a result
of the preaching of Paul and Barnabas on the former
missionary journey, mother and son had passed from
devout Judaism to the Christian faith, and the son
came to be highly honoured by the Christians of
more than one city. St Paul now resolved to take
this young Timothy with him on his onward journey,
and with this purpose (so the order clearly implies)
he circumcised him in order to avoid giving a handle
for misrepresentation to the Jews of those parts. In
everything but the external rite Timothy was a *bona
fide* Jew. If he was to go forth to stand by St Paul's
side in Jewish synagogues as Barnabas the Levite
had done, to have let him remain uncircumcised
would have been to court the imputation of taking
advantage of an accident of education to extend to a
Jew the Pauline exemption of Gentiles from circumcision. Yet it was a bold and startling act, and the
fact that St Paul performed it, when he might have
avoided it by choosing some other associate, shews
that he must have had overmastering reasons indeed
for fixing absolutely on this Lycaonian youth for a
place of such peculiar responsibility.

Timothy's original appointment.

What those reasons were Luke does not tell us, beyond the good testimony of Timothy's Christian neighbours. But an early verse (i. 18) of the first Epistle gives the clue. "This charge I commit to thee, my child Timothy, according to the prophecies which led the way to thee, that in them (i.e. in their power) thou mayest war the good warfare, holding faith and a good conscience." "The prophecies which led the way to thee" this (R.V. marg.) is much the most natural rendering of κατὰ τὰς προ-αγούσας ἐπὶ σὲ προφητείας. Doubtless it would be a strong phrase to use if the occasion referred to were the leaving behind at Ephesus, which is indeed by no means suggested by the very general words that follow of the good warfare, faith and a good conscience. But it fits in excellently with what his narrative suggests as at least a probable course of circumstances. The first missionary journey had been inaugurated at Antioch under circumstances of peculiar solemnity in which Paul and Barnabas were jointly charged with a momentous commission. The journey had been rich in fruitful results, which involved the opening up of a whole new world to be leavened by the Gospel ; and the new advance had been ratified after full consideration by the Twelve and by the Ecclesia of Jerusalem. The new journey was pre-ceded apparently by no fresh inauguration ; it came simply from St Paul's spontaneous desire to revisit the Ecclesiae which they had jointly founded. But now the actual journey was begun under the most disheartening circumstances. Barnabas, whose name had originally stood first, had now withdrawn from the work immediately in hand, and St Paul might well feel that, while he must needs go forward, it must be with a sense of foredoomed failure unless the breach in what had been at the outset a Divinely appointed enterprise were in some way closed up by a no less Divine interposition. He had indeed Silas with him : but this was by his own selection, and apparently Silas stood on the same subordinate footing as Mark had originally done (xiii. 5 ὑπηρέτην), though in the course of the journey the difference of footing seems to disappear. St Paul's words in the Epistle suggest that while he was journeying on in some such state of mind as this, mysterious monitions of the kind called prophetic seemed to come to him, whether within his own spirit, or through the lips of Silas, or both ; and that these voices taught him the course to take by which he should at last find a Divinely provided successor to Barnabas. Such prophecies as have been here supposed would in the strictest sense lead the way to Timothy, just as the heavenly voice in the vision seen by Ananias at Damascus led the way to Paul himself in the house of Judas in the street called Straight (ix. 10 f., 17), or the similar voice in the vision seen by Cornelius at

Cæsarea led the way to St Peter in the house of
Simon the Tanner at Joppa. When at last St Paul
reached Derbe and Lystra (κατήντησεν is St Luke's
expressive word, as though these cities were in some
way a goal to him), the testimony which the young
Timothy received from the brethren might well seem
to be a human echo of a Divine choice already no-
tified by prophecy.

But we may reasonably go a step farther. If
St Paul received Timothy as Divinely made the
partner of his work in place of Barnabas, it would be
at least not unnatural that there should be some
repetition of the solemn acts by which human expression had been given to the Divine mission in the
first instance. If this explanation of "the prophecies"
is right, they must on the one hand have in substance
included some such message as " Separate for me
Timothy for the work whereunto I have called him";
and on the other hand that separation or consecration
would naturally take outward form in fasting and
prayer and laying on of hands by the representatives
of the Lycaonian Ecclesiae, in repetition of what had
been done at Antioch (xiii. 3). In this case however
one additional element would be present, viz. the
special relation in which St Paul stood to Timothy :
he was Timothy's father in the faith, and his subsequent language shews that this essential fact was
to be of permanent significance. It would be natural
therefore that as Jewish Rabbis laid hands on their

disciples, after the example of Moses and Joshua, so
not only the representatives of the Lycaonian Ecclesiae
but also St Paul himself should lay hands on the
disciple and spiritual son now admitted to share his
peculiar commission.

Timothy's χάρισμα.

Taking with us these antecedents, we shall be in a
better position to understand the verse (iv. 14) in
which St Paul bids Timothy, " Neglect not the
gracious gift (χαρίσματος) which is in thee, which was
given thee (διὰ προφητείας), through prophecy with
laying on of the hands of the body of Elders (τοῦ
πρεσβυτερίου). In i. 18 τὰς προαγούσας ἐπί σε
προφητείας would be an extraordinary phrase to
describe prophecies the purpose of which was to
induce St Paul to leave behind him at Ephesus his
coadjutor and often companion of many years; while
Luke's narrative in Acts xvi. enables it to be so interpreted as to give each word exact force; and if the
prophecies of i. 18 are the prophecies which accompanied the early part of St Paul's second journey, it
must be at least worth while to consider whether the
reference is different in iv. 14. Now if we think of
St Paul's own account of Timothy's present mission at
Ephesus, and its temporary and as it were occasional
character, we must see that a laying on of hands by
the Ephesian elders (and it is difficult to think of any
others on this supposition) would be scarcely a

probable though no doubt a possible act under the circumstances, and the addition of prophecy does but increase the incongruity.

If, however, the body of Elders meant was that formed by the Elders of Timothy's own city or neighbourhood, as representing the Ecclesia which sent him forward in conjunction with St Paul to win new regions for the Gospel, the προφητεία spoken of is likewise explained by the prophecies of i. 18.

So too what is said of the χάρισμα or gracious gift of God in Timothy, which had been given him by prophecy with the laying on of hands, harmonises well on this view with the idea running through all the Pauline uses of the word χάρισμα. It was a special gift of God, a special fitness bestowed by Him to enable Timothy to fulfil a distinctive function. Speaking generally the base of this function was preaching the Gospel to those who had not yet heard it, the work of an Evangelist. But it was further limited by the peculiar circumstances : Timothy was to be not merely an Evangelist, but St Paul's special associate in *his* quite unique evangelistic work.

In its origin it was apparently a substitute for the function discharged by Barnabas on the first journey. But owing to the difference of age and personal history between Barnabas and Timothy it must from the first have involved a subordination to St Paul which did not exist in the case of Barnabas. And on the other hand the vast increase in both the range

and the importance of St Paul's personal work
brought about by the force of circumstances since
that time involved a corresponding expansion in the
responsibilities laid on Timothy. An expansion but
not a change of characteristics. It was still the
original χάρισμα to and in Timothy which St Paul
would fitly desire Timothy to kindle anew.

In the second Epistle (i. 6) a similar admonition is
couched in partly different language. Here St Paul
passes from a thanksgiving to the God to whom he
has himself done service as his forefathers had done
(ἀπὸ προγόνων) in a pure conscience, to the thought
of the channels through which Timothy had in like
manner inherited his unfeigned faith, his grandmother
Lois and his mother Eunice. Then from this foundation laid in Timothy's childhood he seems to pass
to that which had been built upon it. "For which
cause (i.e. because I am persuaded that in thee also
dwells unfeigned faith) I put thee in remembrance
to wake into life (ἀναζωπυρεῖν) the χάρισμα of God,
which is in thee by the laying on of my hands : for God
gave us (you Timothy and me Paul, us the heralds of
His Gospel) not a spirit of fearfulness but of power
and of love and of chastened mind. Be not therefore
ashamed of the testimony (μαρτύριον, usually testimony
in act) of our Lord nor of me His prisoner, but suffer
hardship with the Gospel" &c. Here the context
excludes the thought of a χάρισμα meant specially
for Ephesian administration or teaching, to which

there is no allusion whatever. The antecedents of
Timothy's χάρισμα lay in the atmosphere of unfeigned
faith in which he had been bred up, a faith doubtless
constantly put to severe trial through his mother's
position as the wife of a heathen ; and the waking of
Timothy's χάρισμα into fresh life now desired by
St Paul was to shew itself in a spirit which should
animate Timothy's whole personal being.

It is therefore no wonder that in this second
Epistle the laying on of hands of which he speaks is
the laying on of his own hands. In 1 Timothy, the
Epistle which teaches how men ought to behave
themselves in an Ecclesia of a living God, it was
natural, especially in the immediate context of iv. 14,
that St Paul should make mention of the laying on of
hands of the body of Elders of the Ecclesia which
then sent Timothy forth. But in the second Epistle
the personal relation between the two men is everything ; and so the human instrumentality to which he
here refers, the reception of the χάρισμα or gracious
gift which he [here] first describes emphatically as
"the gracious gift of God," is that act, the traditional
symbol of blessing, by which he, already Timothy's
father in the faith and henceforth to have Timothy
always joined with him as also a younger brother, had
borne his part in solemnly inaugurating the beginning
of his new career of duty.

No passages in the least like those which we have

been now examining occur in the Epistle to Titus.
It is no doubt possible that this is due to accident.
But it cannot be said that this Epistle is poor in
contexts when such passages would be quite in place,
supposing them to refer to matters concerning Titus
as much as Timothy. It is moreover remarkable that
language so similar should be found in quite different
contexts in two Epistles, themselves so differing in
character as 1 and 2 Timothy. All these circumstances however explain themselves naturally if the
passages in the two Epistles to Timothy refer to a
single absolutely exceptional solemn act by which
the one man Timothy received a commission to go
forth as St Paul's chosen colleague, because a prophetic oracle had singled him out for this unique
function.

LECTURE XII.

OFFICERS OF THE ECCLESIA IN THE PASTORAL EPISTLES.

FROM Titus and Timothy themselves we pass naturally to the officers of the Ecclesiae of which they were set for a time in charge.

In Crete, as we saw before, there were apparently no Elders previously; and the duty most definitely named as laid on Titus was to set (or establish or appoint) Elders in the several cities. The verb καθίστημι is used in Acts vi. 3 for the Apostles setting or appointing the Seven over the business of attending to the widows of the Greek speaking part of the community at Jerusalem: it is a word implying an exercise of authority, but has no technical force. In 1 and 2 Timothy it is not used, nor any other word approximately similar in sense.

The qualifications of an Elder in Crete.

The first qualifications mentioned (Titus i. 5—9) are not capacities but, so to speak, primary moral conditions affecting men's personal or family relations, "if a man is under no charge or accusation (ἀνέγκλητος, probably not 'blameless' but 'unblamed'), the husband of one wife, having children that believe (i.e. Christian), who are not accused of riotous living, or, unruly.

Then St Paul goes on, Δεῖ γὰρ τὸν ἐπίσκοπον ἀνέγκλητον εἶναι, "For the ἐπίσκοπος must needs be under no charge." It is now pretty generally recognized by those who [do] not break up the Pastoral Epistles into fragments that we have not here a different office, held by one person in contrast to the plural 'Elders,' a view which implies an incredible laxity in St Paul's use of particles. But it is hardly less erroneous to take ἐπίσκοπος as merely a second title, capable of being used convertibly with πρεσβύτερος. In examining the language of Acts xx. we found reason to think that when St Paul, addressing at Miletus those who in *v.* 17 are called the Elders of the (Ephesian) Ecclesia, says, "take heed to yourselves and to all the flock in which the Holy Spirit set you as ἐπισκόπους," he used this word as descriptive, not as a second title, so that we might render it "set you to have oversight." It is exactly the same here, only on clearer evidence. If ἐπίσκοπον is a title of office, the article before it is without motive, and ἀνέγκλητον εἶναι following it is a tame repetition when εἴ τις ἐστὶν ἀνέγκλητος has preceded. But taken descriptively it supplies a link which gives force to every other word. 'A man who is to be made an Elder should be one who is ἀνέγκλητος, *for* (γάρ) he that hath oversight must needs be ἀνέγκλητος as a steward of God.' 'Elder' is the title, 'oversight' is the function to be exercised by the holder of the title within the Ecclesia. The nature of the oversight is not defined except as being that exercised by a steward in a household of God. But, as we saw before, the general conception of the word is closely akin to that suggested by the pastoral relation, if we are to take as our guides the usage of the LXX. the Apocrypha and Philo, and especially 1 Pet. ii. 25 τὸν ποιμένα καὶ ἐπίσκοπον τῶν ψυχῶν ὑμῶν.

Then follow five negative moral qualifications, " not' self-willed, not soon angry, not given to wine, no striker, not greedy of filthy lucre "; then six positive moral qualifications (the first alone worthy of special comment), "given to hospitality (lit. a lover of strangers, φιλόξενον), a lover of good, soberminded, just, holy, temperate."

Last comes a quite different qualification, "holding fast (if that is the meaning here of the difficult word ἀντεχόμενον) by the word which is faithful according to the teaching (διδαχήν), that he may be able both to exhort in the doctrine (διδασκαλία) that is healthful and to convict the gainsayers." Without pausing at the various difficulties of this verse, we can see that at least it requires in the Cretan Elders a hold on Christian principles of at least morality or religion, such as would enable them to give hortatory instruction of a salutary kind to all, and likewise to give competent answers to gainsayers, who are described more particularly in the following verses. On "the doctrine that is healthful" I may be able to say a word farther on[1]. It is clear that St Paul here contemplates his Elders as having (at least normally) an office of teaching, both of a positive and of a negative kind. Apart from this, and from what may be included in the comprehensive words 'having oversight,' it is difficult to find any distinctive characteristics mentioned. The moral qualities, positive and negative, are such as men officially representing the Ecclesia and having charge of its members would be expected to shew more than other men. But they are no less among the obvious qualities to be looked for in all members of the community. If hospitality seems at first sight a virtue specially pertaining to the leading men of the Ecclesia, we must also remember how it is inculcated on all alike in Rom. xii. 13, 1 Pet. iv. 9, Heb. xiii. 2. Respecting any other officers than the Elders Titus receives no directions.

[1] See p. 220.

Elders in Ephesus according to 1 *Timothy.*

The same subject is approached in a very different way in 1 Tim., as might be expected from the different circumstances. The earlier of the specific charges given by St Paul to Timothy, which begin with chap. ii., will need a word further on. Having spoken on prayer, and on men and women, St Paul comes in iii. 1 to another theme affecting the Ephesian Ecclesia, "If any man seeketh after ἐπι- σκοπῆς (a function of oversight), he desireth a good work. He therefore that hath oversight must needs be free from reproach (δεῖ οὖν τὸν ἐπίσκοπον ἀνεπί- λημπτον εἶναι)." So I think we should naturally interpret the words in any case on account of the article. But if the passage stood alone we could not tell whether the office intended was one held by one person or by many, and the influence of later usage might naturally suggest that it was held by *one*, i.e. was what we call an episcopate. In v. 17 ff. there are some secondary references to Elders, but nothing to shew either identity with the ἐπίσκοπος of chap. iii. or their difference. Again the seven careful verses on him that hath oversight (iii. 1—7) are followed by six equally careful verses on διάκονοι, whom we may for convenience call 'deacons'. Now if the ἐπίσκοπος of this Epistle were a single officer, superior to all others, the only way of accounting for St Paul's passing next to the διάκονοι, neglecting the Elders here, and dealing

with them in a quite different way farther on, would
be to suppose, as some have of late on other grounds
supposed, that the ἐπίσκοπος and διάκονοι exercised
one kind of functions and the Elders exercised another
altogether different. But none of these suppositions
can stand in the face of Tit. i., for the correspondence
of language forbids us to give the word an essentially
different sense in the two passages. It follows that
the two consecutive careful passages in iii. refer
to Elders and to διάκονοι respectively, and that the
references to Elders by name in chap. v. are, as we
should expect, practically supplementary in character.

In this Epistle Paul is not providing for the
institution of an order of Elders but giving instruction
respecting a long existing order. Throughout these
verses (iii. 1—13) there is not a word addressed to
Timothy, directing him what he himself should do
in respect of men holding these offices. There is
simply, as in all the earlier part of the Epistle, a
setting forth in general terms of what ought to be.
But it is remarkable how considerably the qualifications recited here agree in essentials with the
qualifications laid down in respect of Crete, though
there are many differences both of words and of arrangement. The only negative qualities here mentioned are " no brawler (violent, petulant person), no
striker"; the omissions generically being of fundamental qualities too obvious to be forgotten at

Ephesus, such as the final triad "righteous, holy, temperate"; while the moral qualities now added are of the calm and peaceful type. The long final clause of Titus about teaching is replaced by the single word διδακτικόν, "apt to teach," in the middle of the list, following "a lover of hospitality", while at the end of this list stands now the clause "one that ruleth well his own house, having his children in subjection with all gravity" (expounded further in the next verse). Then come two other qualifications, one negative, "no novice (νεόφυτον), lest he be puffed up," etc.; and one positive, in a separate sentence, "Moreover he must be well witnessed of by them that are without," etc., an emphatic expansion and extension of the first requirement, that he be without reproach. Here too we learn singularly little about the actual functions, except what is contained in the former word 'oversight', and in the phrase "have charge (ἐπιμελήσεται) of an Ecclesia of God." Doubtless it was superfluous to mention either the precise functions or the qualifications needed for definitely discharging them. What was less obvious and more important was the danger lest official excellencies of one kind or another should cloak the absence of Christian excellencies. To St Paul the representative character, so to speak, of those who had oversight in the Ecclesia, their conspicuous embodiment of what the Ecclesia itself was meant to shew itself, was a more important thing than any acts or teachings by which their oversight could be formally exercised.

Before we consider the διάκονοι who are mentioned next, it will be best to take what further is said of the Elders in chap. v. The 'Elder' of *v.* 1 is doubtless one so called not for any office or function but merely for age. It is otherwise in *vv.* 17, 18, " Let the Elders that preside excellently (καλῶς προεστῶτες) be counted worthy of double honour, especially they that labour (κοπιῶντες, i.e. not merely work, but work laboriously) in speech and teaching; for the Scripture saith, 'Thou shalt not muzzle an ox that treadeth out the corn' and 'The labourer is worthy of his hire.'" This word 'προεστῶτες' standing at the head, includes more than "ruling" (so all English versions). The sentence implies that this was a function common to all the Elders. Those who discharged it not merely well (εὖ) but καλῶς, excellently, are to be esteemed worthy of double honour, an honour exceeding that due to their office; and such honour, he hints, should be shown by a care on the part of the Ecclesia not to neglect the maintenance of those who labour on its behalf. Special honour, St Paul adds, is due to those Elders, coming under this description, who labour in speech and teaching. The distinction implies with tolerable certainty that teaching was not a universal function of the Elders of Ephesus. On the other hand, the language used does *not* suggest that there

were two separate and well-defined classes, teaching
Elders and non-teaching Elders. Teaching was doubtless the most important form in which guidance and
superintendence were exercised. But to all appearance the Ephesian Ecclesia used freely the services of
men who had no special gift of this kind, but who
were well qualified to act as Elders in other respects.

Then in *v.* 19 comes the converse case of Elders
worthy not of praise but of blame. First, an Elder's
office and position should secure him against coming
into suspicion through mere random talk : Timothy,
now first addressed directly in this connexion, was
to give attention to no accusation which was not
supported by the security provided by the Jewish
law in accordance with manifest justice, the testimony
of three or at the least two witnesses. On the other
hand, those who sinned (in this context it can hardly
be doubted that the reference is to *Elders* who sinned)
Timothy was to rebuke publicly, that the rest also
might have fear.

In all this Timothy is manifestly clothed for the
time with a paramount authority, doubtless as the
temporary representative of St Paul guided by St –
Paul's instructions, St Paul himself having the authority of a founder, and that founder one who had
seen the Lord Jesus. But he is not content to leave
these instructions about Elders without a further
warning. In an adjuration of peculiar solemnity, as
though guarding against a danger which might only

too easily invade Timothy, he charges him against letting himself be guided in these matters by any *praejudicium*, and especially against meting out honour or censure on the ground of his own personal preferences.

What is required of 'Deacons.'

Returning now to chap. iii., after the seven verses on "him that hath oversight," viz. one of the presbyters, we read in a sentence which has no principal verb (the δεῖ εἶναι being carried on from ii.), "Διάκονοι in like manner [must be] grave, not double-tongued[1]," διλόγους, not addicted to much wine, not given to filthy lucre, having the secret of their faith in a pure conscience [said probably with special reference to their opportunities for dishonest gain]; and let these also [these διάκονοι, no less than the Elders] first be proved, then let them minister (act as διάκονοι) if they lie under no accusation. Then comes, "Women in like manner (evidently not as A.V. the wives of διάκονοι, but as Bishop Lightfoot shewed forcibly some years ago at a Diocesan Conference, women who are διάκονοι), grave, not backbiters, sober (probably as Bishop Ellicott in the literal sense, νηφαλίους), faithful in all things." These four qualities are either repetitions or characteristic modifications of the four moral qualities required for

---

[1] Or perhaps 'tale-bearers'; see Lightfoot on *Polyc.* 5.

men who are διάκονοι; gravity (σεμνότης) being
required of both, freedom from backbiting answering
to freedom from talebearing, soberness, freedom from
addiction to much wine, and faithfulness or trustworthiness in all things to freedom from filthy lucre.
Then St Paul returns once more to the men διάκονοι
in order to lay stress on the importance of their
conduct of their own family relations. " Let διάκονοι
be husbands of one wife, ruling (or guiding, προϊστά-
μενοι) their children well and their own households.
For they that have ministered (served as διάκονοι)
well gain to themselves a good standing (βαθμόν) and
great boldness in the power of faith, even the faith
that is in Christ Jesus."

This is all that we learn about διάκονοι from the
Pastoral Epistles. The Epistle to Titus in prescribing
the appointment of Elders says nothing about διάκονοι.
Probably the Christian communities of Crete were
not yet mature enough to make the institution as
yet desirable.

Taking the six verses together, it is clear that we
have to do not with mere voluntary rendering
services of whatsoever kind, but with a definite class
of men, not merely ministering to the Ecclesia or its
members but formally recognised by the Ecclesia as
having an office of this kind. This is implied partly
in the parallelism to the Elders just above, partly in
the imperative form, partly in the requirement of
probation, whether that means probation in the work

itself or careful examination of qualifications and antecedents. The moral requirements are substantially the same as for the Elders, so far as they go, except that these alone include the absence of talebearing for the men, backbiting for the women, faults which evidently might easily have place in men who came much in contact with various individual Christians and families, but less so in men entrusted with oversight and teaching. On the other hand we find nothing corresponding to three marked qualifications of Elders, viz. cheerful hospitality, capacity for teaching, and freedom from reproach or accusation, to say nothing of positive good testimony from outsiders, while on the other hand equal stress is laid in the two cases on the domestic qualifications implied in " a husband of one wife" (however we interpret this ambiguous phrase) and in " excellent control of children and household." Evidently a man whose own family constituted a bad example for the rest of the community was to be held disqualified for either kind of office in the Ecclesia, whatever his personal capacities might be. It is a striking illustration of what is practically taught by many parts of the Apostolic Epistles, that the true Ecclesiastical life and the true Christian life and the true human life are all one and the same. To return to the three omissions. The silence about freedom from reproach or accusation in the case of the διάκονοι explains itself if their work, unlike the Elders', had usually little publicity or conspicuousness. So

too the silence about hospitality is natural for men
whose place in the Ecclesia did not seem to impose
this as a duty upon them more than on the members
of the community generally. The silence about
teaching may in like manner be safely taken as
sufficient evidence that teaching formed no part of
the duty of a διάκονος.

The clause "holding the mystery of the faith in
a pure conscience," cannot when carefully examined,
be safely interpreted as having reference to a mystery
of doctrine which they are to 'hold' in the sense of
'holding fast.' Τὸ μυστήριον τῆς πίστεως, undoubtedly
a difficult phrase, is probably (as Weiss explains it)
the secret constituted by their own inner faith, not
known to men but inspiring all their work ; and then
the stress lies on "in a pure conscience" (see the
association of faith and a pure or good conscience in
i. 5, 19). Thus in this clause a true inward religion
and a true inward morality are laid down as required
for the office of διάκονοι ; that is, the external nature
of the services chiefly rendered by them was not to
be taken as sanctioning any merely external efficiency.
The lowest service to be rendered to the Ecclesia and
to its members would be a delusive and dangerous
service if rendered by men, however otherwise active,
who were not themselves moved by the faith on
which the Ecclesia rested and governed by its
principles. This however has nothing to do with
teaching on the part of the διάκονοι, to which there is

no reference in the whole passage.   On the other
hand we may safely say that it would have been
contrary to the spirit of the Apostolic age to *prohibit*
all teaching on the part of any διάκονοι who had
real capacity of that kind.   But this would be no part
of their official duty, and so it naturally finds no
mention here.

The last verse, iii. 13, has been often understood
to say that excellent discharge of the duties of a
διάκονος would rightly entitle him to promotion to a
higher kind of work, doubtless that of an Elder.
Βαθμός undeniably means a step, and so might easily
be used for a grade of dignity and function.   But the
rest of the verse renders this interpretation unnatural;
and the true sense doubtless is that διάκονοι by excellent discharge of their duties may win for themselves
an excellent vantage ground, a "standing" (R.V.) a
little, as it were, above the common level, enabling
them to exercise an influence and moral authority to
which their work *as such* could not entitle them.

The words διάκονος *and* διακονία.

We must turn now to the word or words by which
their function is designated.   The primary sense of
διάκονος, as it meets us in Greek prose literature
generally, is a servant or slave within the household,
whose chief duty consists in waiting on his master at
table, and sometimes in marketing for him.   Originally perhaps he was a messenger: but if so, that

sense was at least too obsolete long before the Christian era to be important to us. Further, to Greek[1] ears the word almost always seems to suggest relatively low kinds of offices, whether rendered (in the literal original sense) to a master, or (figuratively) to a state. Our word 'menial' nearly answers to the sense thus practically predominant. It is a strange mistake of Archbishop Trench's (his article on this word and its synonyms being indeed altogether less careful than usual) to say that διάκονος does not represent the servant in his relation to a person. The true proper Greek sense is preserved in several places of the Gospels, e.g. Lk. xii. 37, "he shall gird himself, and make them sit down to meat, and shall come and *serve them*" (διακονήσει αὐτοῖς) ; or again, xxii. 26 f. And this last passage leads to what is really the same sense in the great saying (Mt. xx. 28 ‖ Mk.), "The Son of man came not to be ministered unto but to minister."

One great exception there is to the Greek contempt for all pertaining to a διάκονος, but it is an exception in appearance only, it is used of Athenian statesmen who had saved their country. Aristeides[2]

---

[1] Two or three passages of Plato in particular bring out the association connected with it : *Gorg.* 518 A, 521 A; *Rep.* 370 f. In *Gorg.* 518 A we have the significant series of epithets δουλοπρεπεῖς τε καὶ διακονικὰς καὶ ἀνελευθέρους. There are clear echoes of these passages in the same sense long after in Plut. *Mor.* II. 794 A and Aristeid. *Orat.* 46 (pp. 152 f., 187, 193), and doubtless elsewhere; and the same feeling shews itself in a number of passages in Aristotle's *Politics*.

[2] *Orat.* 46, pp. 198 f.

refuses to call them διάκονοι of the state, but will gladly call them διάκονοι of the Saviour Gods who had used their instrumentality; and in several remarkable passages Epictetus (Diss. iii. 22, 69; 24, 65; iv. 7, 20; cf. iii. 26, 28) makes it the truest dignity of a man to be a διάκονος of God. The Gospel gave the word a still higher consecration of the same kind. The Christian, even more than the Jew, felt himself to be the servant of a heavenly Lord, nay of a Lord who had taken on Himself the form of a servant; and thus for Him every grade and pattern of service was lifted into a higher sphere. It would be superfluous to enumerate the passages in which men are called διάκονοι of God or of Christ, the least obvious being Rom. xiii. 4, when the civil magistrate bears this title. Ministration thus became one of the primary aims of all Christian actions (cf. Eph. iv. 12; 1 Pet. iv. 10 f.; 1 Cor. xii. 5; Rom. xii. 7). Apostleship, the highest form of ministration, is repeatedly designated thus (Acts i. 17, 25; xx. 24; xxi. 19; 2 Cor. iv. 1; v. 18; vi. 3 (cf. 4); Rom. xi. 13); sometimes with the special reference ministration "of the Gospel" (Eph. iii. 7; Col. i. 23); or "of the Ecclesia" (Col. i. 25). But naturally Apostleship does not stand alone in this respect. In 1 Cor. iii. 5 St Paul calls Apollos and himself alike διάκονοι through whose instrumentality the Corinthians had believed. In 2 Tim. iv. 5 Timothy is bidden, "Be thou sober in all things, suffer hardship, do the work of an evangelist, bring to fulfilment (πληροφόρησον) thy ministration"; and the Colossian Christians (Col. iv. 17) are bidden to tell Archippus, "Look to the ministration which thou receivedst in the Lord, that thou fulfil it" (πληροῖς).

Again, there are a few passages in which the words are used very differently, viz. for ministrations rendered not to God but to St Paul himself. Thus Acts xix. 22 calls Timothy and Erastus δύο τῶν διακονούντων αὐτῷ on the occasion of his sending them forward from Ephesus to Macedonia. It is probably in the same sense that Tychicus is called not only a beloved brother but a faithful διάκονος in the Lord (Eph. vi. 21 ; Col. iv. 7). So in 2 Tim. (iv. 11) St Paul calls Mark right useful to himself εἰς διακονίαν, and tells Philemon (13) how he had purposed to keep with him Onesimus ἵνα ὑπὲρ σοῦ μοι διακονῇ in the bonds of the Gospel ; and appeals to Timothy's knowledge (2 Tim. i. 18) how great had been the ministrations of Onesiphorus at Ephesus, evidently (as the context shews) chiefly though perhaps not exclusively to St Paul himself.

It is doubtful whether this last ministration of Onesiphorus to St Paul was by public labours of some kind or by personal attendance and help to St Paul as a man. At all events this latter sense is likewise amply represented in the Acts and Epistles with reference to the supply of material wants, thus connecting itself directly with what we saw to be the

most exact sense of these words in Greek daily life.
A specially interesting passage for our purpose is
Acts vi. 1, 2, 6, the account of the institution of the
Seven at Jerusalem. The widows of the Greek-
speaking Jews, we hear, had been neglected (ἐν τῇ
διακονίᾳ τῇ καθημερινῇ), the daily provision of food
for the poor at a common table. The Twelve object
to leaving the Word of God in order διακονεῖν
τραπέζαις, and propose by the appointment of the
Seven to be able to devote themselves to prayer and
τῇ διακονίᾳ τοῦ λόγου. This last phrase is probably
used in intentional antithesis to the ministration of
tables or of meat and drink, to indicate that the
Twelve were not refusing to accept the evangelical
function of ministering, but only to neglect the ministration of the higher sustenance for the sake of the
lower sustenance. In Acts xi. 29, xii. 25, the mission
of Barnabas and Saul from Antioch to carry help to
the brethren of Judea in the famine is called a διακονία;
and St Paul himself several times uses the same word,
usually with τοῖς ἁγίοις or εἰς τοὺς ἁγίους added, for
the Gentile collections for a similar purpose which
occupied so much of his thoughts at a later time
(Rom. xv. 25, 31; 2 Cor. viii. 4; ix. 1, 12, 13).

Another instructive passage is 1 Cor. xvi. 15,
" Now I beseech you, brethren (ye know the house of
Stephanas, that it is a firstfruit of Achaia, and [that]
they laid themselves out εἰς διακονίαν τοῖς ἁγίοις),—
[I beseech you] that ye also be subject (ὑποτάσσησθε)

to such, and to everyone that helpeth in the work and laboureth." These words suggest that Stephanas was a wealthy or otherwise influential Corinthian who with his household made it his aim to use his position for the benefit of Christians travelling to Corinth from a distance, all of whom in Apostolic language were saints or holy, as all alike members of a holy community, and consecrated to a holy life. Services like these rendered by a man of social eminence made it good for the members of the Corinthian Ecclesia to look up to him as a leader. He was in fact affording an example of what St Paul meant by ὁ προϊστάμενος in Rom. xii. 8. The same kind of service is implied under other words in what is said of Prisca and Aquila in Rom. xvi. 3 f. And so we come to Phœbe, the subject of the two preceding verses, Rom. xvi. 1 f. "But I commend to you," St Paul writes, " Phœbe our sister, who is also a διάκονος of the Ecclesia that is at Cenchreæ; that ye receive her in the Lord worthily of the saints, and that ye assist her in whatsoever matter she may have need of you : for she herself also shewed herself a προστάτις (patroness) of many, and of mine own self." These last words shew pretty plainly that Phœbe was a lady of wealth, or position. She had been a προστάτις of many, including St Paul. It is most unlikely that St Paul would have applied to her a word suggestive of the kind of help and encouragement given by wealthy benevolent people to dependents or helpless strangers if she had been only a humble member of the community, who shewed kindness to other Christians no more favourably placed. We may safely conclude that what Stephanas had done at Corinth *she* had done at Cenchreæ, its seaport on the east, nine miles off. But if this was her position, it is certainly possible, but hardly likely, that διάκονον τῆς ἐκκλησίας etc. means "a deaconess of the Ecclesia that is at Cenchreæ." The καὶ before διάκονον, which is almost certainly genuine, points likewise to this term as conveying not a mere fact about Phœbe but a second ground of commendation parallel to her being one whom St Paul admitted to the distinction of being called his sister (as he spoke of Timothy and others as ὁ ἀδελφός). Hence we may naturally take it in the ordinary, not the later technical sense, as one who ministered to the Ecclesia at Cenchreæ, the nature of the ministration being described in the next verse. To call her a διάκονον meant thus what was meant by saying that the house of Stephanas laid themselves out εἰς διακονίαν. One passage more, from a later writer, remains. The Hebrews are assured (Heb. vi. 10) that "God will not forget their work and the love which they shewed, looking unto His name, in that they had ministered to the saints, and still did minister."

The function of 'Deacons' in Ephesus.

It can hardly be doubted that the officers of the
Ephesian ἐκκλησία, who in 1 Tim. are called διάκονοι,
had for their work in like manner, chiefly, perhaps
even exclusively, the help of a material kind which
the poorer or more helpless members of the body
received from the community at large. It is difficult
to account for the word, used thus absolutely, in any
other way. They would share with the Elders the
honour and blessing of being recognised ministers of
the Ecclesia. But that would be nothing distinctive.
Ministration to the bodily wants of its needy members
would be distinctive, and would obviously tally with
the associations most familiar to Greek ears in
connexion with the word. The analogy of the Seven
at Jerusalem points the same way. There is, of
course, no evidence for historical continuity between
the Seven and either the Ephesian διάκονοι or the
developed order of Deacons of later times. The New
Testament gives not the slightest indication of any
connexion. But the Seven at Jerusalem would of
course be well known to St Paul and to many others
outside Palestine, and it would not be strange if the
idea propagated itself. Indeed analogous wants
might well lead to analogous institutions. There is
very little reason to think that the διάκονοι of 1 Tim.
had its origin in Jewish usage. Some critics have
been attracted by the similarity of title for the

Ḥazân hakknêseth, or servant of the synagogue. He is doubtless the official called ὑπηρέτης in Luke iv. 20. Now ὑπηρέτης and διάκονος are often used interchangeably (though ὑπηρέτης is the vaguer word of the two), and Epiph. 135 A speaks of ʿΑζανιτῶν τῶν παρ᾽ αὐτοῖς διακόνων ἑρμηνευομένων ἢ ὑπηρετῶν. But the duties of the Ḥazân were different, and apparently confined to the walls of the synagogue. Still less could the office have had a heathen origin, despite the two inscriptions cited by Hatch p. 50, C.I.G. 1793 b. add. at Anactorium in Acarnania, where διάκονος is one of ten offices evidently connected with sacrificial feasts, standing between μάγειρος and ἀρχοι-νοχοῦς ; and 3037 at Metropolis in Lydia, where twice over we have a ἱερεύς, a ἱερεία, a (female) διάκονος, and two (male) διάκονοι.

In the Apostolic conception of an Ecclesia such a function as that of these Ephesian διάκονοι had a sufficiently lofty side ; the διάκονοι were the main instruments for giving practical effect to the mutual sympathy of the members of the body.

Had then the word already become technical when 1 Tim. was written? It is not easy to answer quite precisely. We cannot safely argue back from later usage without knowing whether later usage was affected by this very passage. But the office can hardly have been without a title from the first, and no other title for the office occurs in the Epistle, while St Paul evidently assumed no other designation or description to be necessary. It seems pretty certain, therefore, that διάκονος was already a recognised title among the Christians of Ephesus. On the other hand it seems equally probable that in this context St Paul uses it with express reference to its ordinary associations in antithesis to ἐπισκοπῆς and ἐπίσκοπον above. That is, he treats the two offices as characteristically offices, the one of government, the other of the reverse of government 'service'. How natural this contrast would seem to Greeks we can readily see by a passage of Aeschines (*c. Ctesiph.* 13) respecting the classification of public offices at Athens according to the authorities which elected or nominated to them. Thus tested, the lower class of offices, he says, is not an ἀρχή but ἐπιμελεία τις καὶ διακονία, and similarly, further on, he uses the phrase οὐ διακονεῖν ἀλλ' ἄρχειν. Assuredly the ἐπισκοπή of the Elders would count as an ἀρχή or government, and thus the contrast would need no explicit comment.

The salutation in Phil. i. 1.

Let us now return for a moment to the salutation of Philippians, which it would have been unsatisfactory to consider in detachment from the illustration afforded by the Pastoral Epistles. "Paul and Timothy, servants of Christ Jesus to all the saints in Christ Jesus that are at Philippi, σὺν ἐπισκόποις καὶ διακόνοις." If the verse stood alone, no one would hesitate before assuming that these are two titles of

14—2

two offices, ἐπίσκοποι and διάκονοι. Of course it would not follow that ἐπισκόποις bears here its later monarchical sense : the plural (being addressed to a single Ecclesia) and what is known of the arrangements of the Apostolic age generally would shew the office to be one shared by at least a plurality of persons in the same Ecclesia. But then we have to face the fact that this Epistle stands chronologically between St Paul's words at Miletus and his letter to Titus and 1 Tim., which agree in using ἐπίσκοπος, not as a title synonymous with the title πρεσβύτερος, Elder, but as a word describing the function of the persons entitled Elders. In other words, ἐπισκόποις, if a title in Philipp. i. 1, would imply a more advanced state of things than that of the Pastoral Epistles. The clue to what seems the right interpretation is given by those thirteen verses of 1 Tim. iii. which we were considering lately. St Paul does not mean simply two different offices, but two contrasted offices, or (to speak more correctly) two contrasted functions, "with them that have oversight, and them that do service [minister]." On the common view he would be simply sending salutations to the two sets of men independently of the salutation to the 'saints' at Philippi generally : and in that case we might find it hard to explain why such a salutation is withheld in writing to other Ecclesiae. In reality he is probably thinking less of the men coming under either head than of the Ecclesia as a whole : these two functions are to him the main outward manifestations that the community of saints was indeed an organised body, needing and possessing government on the one side and service on the other. It would matter little how many offices there were, with or without titles, two, or three, or twenty. That was a matter of external arrangement, which might vary endlessly according to circumstances. The essential thing was to recognise the need of the two fundamental types of function.

It might perhaps be suggested that sufficient account has not here been taken of the usage of early Christian writers outside the New Testament. But the fact is, their evidence is of little help. To the best of my belief the only place where ἐπίσκοποι *alone* is used of Elders is in the Didache 15, " Choose therefore for yourselves to be ἐπισκόπους καὶ διακόνους men worthy of the Lord, meek, not lovers of money, etc."; where the precise nature of the usage is as ambiguous as in Philippians, from which Epistle indeed the combination is probably borrowed, whether rightly understood or not. On the other hand both Clement and Hermas use both ἐπίσκοπος and πρεσβύτερος, and apparently in just the same way as St Paul at Miletus and in the Pastoral Epistles : in Clem. 44 τοῦ ὀνόματος τῆς ἐπισκοπῆς, as both Lightfoot and Harnack rightly assume, does not mean the title ἐπίσκοπος but the dignity attaching to the function of ἐπισκοπή, according to the frequent biblical sense of 'name'.

'Laying on of hands' in 1 *Tim.* v. 22.

We have not quite done with the Pastoral Epistles, though nearly so. One verse should be mentioned here, because it has been so often understood in a sense bearing on this subject of offices in the Ecclesia, v. 22, "Lay hands hastily on no one, neither be in fellow- ship with sins of others : keep thyself pure." This verse stands next to the adjuration against the shewing of favour or prejudice by Timothy in his sanctioning special honour for some Elders, and him- self receiving accusations and uttering rebukes in the case of others. It is followed by the verse bidding Timothy be no longer a water-drinker. Thus it stands between five verses relating to Elders and a single verse relating to Timothy's own imprudent adoption of a questionable form of ἁγνεία or cere- monial purity. In this position the laying on of hands is by most commentators, as also by such Greek fathers as notice the verse, interpreted of or- dination, i.e. of the Elders previously mentioned : the other equally familiar laying on of hands, that con- nected with baptism and eventually known as Confir- mation, being evidently out of place here. This view is certainly possible, but it suits rather imperfectly the strong phrase "be not partaker in sins of others"; and it makes an additional precept about Elders come in *after* that solemn adjuration, the natural place of such a precept being *before* the adjuration. There is

much greater probability in the view taken by some
Latin fathers, by our own Hammond (who defends it
at great length), and by a few recent critics, including
Dr Ellicott, that the laying on of hands, the act
symbolical of blessing, was here the act of blessing by
which penitents were received back into the communion of the faithful (cf. 2 Cor. ii. 6 f.). The
practice was certainly widely spread among Christians
not more than four or five generations later, and as
Hammond points out, the principle of it is involved
in the laying on of hands on the sick accepted from
others and practised by our Lord Himself repeatedly,
as also by St Paul (Acts xxviii. 8), even as by Ananias
in restoring St Paul's own sight (Acts ix. 12, 17), and
probably implied in James v. 14 (προσευξάσθωσαν ἐπ᾽
αὐτόν).

'Laying on of hands' in ordination.

Neither here then nor elsewhere in the New
Testament have we any information about the manner
in which Elders were consecrated or ordained (the
exact word matters little) to their office ; the χειροτονήσαντες of Acts xiv. 23 having of course no
reference to a solemn act of appointment but to the
preceding choice, just as in 2 Cor. viii. 19 χειροτονηθείς
means that Titus had been chosen by the Ecclesiae to
travel with St Paul. The only passages of the New
Testament in which laying on of hands is connected
with an act answering to ordination are four, viz. Acts

vi. 6, the laying on of the hands of the Twelve on the Seven at Jerusalem at their first appointment; Acts xiii. 3, the laying on of the hands of the representatives of the Ecclesia of Antioch on Barnabas and Saul in consequence of a prophetic monition sending them forth; and the two passages about Timothy, likewise, as we have lately seen, due in all probability to another prophetic monition sending him forth on a unique mission intimately connected with that former mission. Jewish usage[1] in the case of Rabbis and their disciples renders it highly probable that (as a matter of fact) laying on of hands was largely practised in the Ecclesiae of the Apostolic age as a rite introductory to ecclesiastical office. But as the New Testament tells us no more than what has been already mentioned, it can hardly be likely that any essential principle was held to be involved in it. It was enough that an Ecclesia should in modern phrase be organised, or in the really clearer Apostolic phrase be treated as a body made up of members with a diversity of functions; and that all things should be done decently and in order.

---

[1] The transference of the Semīchah to the Sanhedrin and Patriarch is of later date: see Hamburger, *Art. Ordinirung* ii. 883 ff.

[The Semīchah was the ceremony accompanying the appointment of a Rabbi and admission to the Sanhedrin. The root Sāmach is used of Moses laying his hands on Joshua at his appointment, Nu. xxvii. 18, 23 and of putting the hand on the sacrifices, Lev. i. 4, iv. 4, etc.

See Buxtorf, *Lex.* 1498. Selden, *de Synedriis* ii. 7.]

We must not stop now to examine the sixteen verses on widows which open chap. v., merely noticing the way in which the Christian community of Ephesus was at this time caring for its most helpless and at the same time deserving members. A widow of at least sixty fulfilling certain moral conditions, among others that of having laid herself out to help other members of the community in their needs, was to be placed on the roll (*v.* 9 καταλεγέσθω), evidently (see *v.* 16) the Ecclesia at large was to be charged with their support.

LECTURE XIII.

BRIEF NOTES ON VARIOUS EPISTLES AND RECAPITULATION.

Directions for public prayer in 1 *Timothy.*

RETURNING for a moment to chap. ii., from the continuation of which in chap. iii. we have already learned so much, we come in its opening verses to the first part of the charge which St Paul was specially desirous to give now to Timothy for his guidance. For the worship of the Ecclesia this charge of intercession (ii. 1—4) takes precedence of all others. These various forms of prayer and thanksgivings are to be offered up by its members, and there is to be no exclusiveness in the subject of them. Christians are to pray not only for Christians and Christian communities, but for all mankind ; then he adds (you will remember that Nero was reigning) " for kings and all that are in high places." The order of society, and those who had (as our Lord told Pilate) received

authority over it from above, were not to be foreign
to Christians' goodwill and prayers, much less to be
hated and prayed against. This last monition repeats
in another shape what had been written by St Paul
to the Romans, the echo of which in few but forcible
words is to be heard from St Peter. It inspires one
of the most striking parts of the magnificent prayer
contained in the newly recovered portion of Clement's
Epistle, and the same strain sounds repeatedly in the
Second Century. But that former monition about
prayer for all mankind, with the reason given for it in
vv. 3, 4, is even more characteristic of St Paul's conception of the function of the Ecclesia in the world.
The prominence of the words meaning 'saving' in the
Pastoral Epistles has often been noticed, and assuredly
it is not accidental. Doubtless the various thoughts relating to Christ's relation to the universe, to humanity,
and to the Ecclesia which found expression in Ephesians, indeed to a certain extent some years before in
Rom. xi., were in themselves likely to deepen and
expand St Paul's sense of saving as the comprehensive
term to describe the Divine action upon and for mankind. But at the time when he wrote the Pastorals he
was further, if I mistake not, under a peculiarly strong
sense of the evil likely to penetrate into the Christians
of Crete and Ephesus from Rabbinism, not from the
old mistaken zeal for Law and Circumcision, but from
the new casuistry and fabling of the Jewish doctors.
This is I believe the key to various peculiarities of

these Epistles, and not least to their frequent insistence on what was healthful ("sound") as opposed to a morbid occupation with unprofitable trifles (1 Tim. vi. 4, νοσῶν περὶ ζητήσεις, etc.). Now one marked characteristic of the rabbinical spirit was its bitter exclusiveness, the exclusiveness of men who, as St Paul told the Thessalonians (1 Thess. ii. 15 f.) were "contrary to all men, forbidding us to speak to the Gentiles that they may be saved." And so St Paul teaches the new Ecclesiae of God that He whom they worship is emphatically the Saviour God, who willeth that all men should be saved and come to the knowledge of truth, and thus leads them to feel that the work of an Ecclesia of His as towards the world is likewise to save ; even as the Gospel which he was himself commissioned to preach to the Gentiles had for its subject Him who had given Himself a ransom not for His chosen people only but for all. This topic may seem not a little remote from the obviously ecclesiastical questions about Elders and Deacons; but it bears very closely on St Paul's conception of a Christian Ecclesia.

Various evidence of James, 1 Peter, Hebrews, Apocalypse.

St James's Epistle will not detain us long. To him the ideal twelve tribes of the ancient Israel, whether in Palestine or in the Dispersion, were still a reality, though doubtless he reckoned none but Christians as

rightly representing them. To the yet wider Christian
Ecclesia he makes no reference. But he shews a true
sense of what was meant by membership of an Ecclesia
in the narrower sense. It is latent in his rebuke of
the old misuse of the poor by the rich in the congregation for worship, still called 'synagogue' (chap. ii.).
It comes out more clearly in the last chapter, where
the fellowship of the whole body in one of its members
who is sick and thus cut off from the rest, is expressed
and made active by the intercessions of those who
are expressly called not simply 'the Elders' but 'the
Elders of the Ecclesia,' in this as in other ways the
vehicles of the sympathy of the whole brotherhood ;
and where again the reality of this fraternal relation is
at once tested and strengthened not only by mutual
intercession but by mutual confession of sins.

St Peter can hardly be said to add any distinctly
new element to what we have already found in St
Paul, unless it be the bold but luminous comparison
by which in ii. 4, 5, instead of filling out the image of
a body with thoughts connected with building, he
boldly substitutes the building as the primary image,
shaping it to his purpose by adding the thought of
living stones "coming to" a living corner-stone. But
he sets forth with special vividness the prerogatives of
God's new or Christian Ecclesia as having now suc-
.ceeded to the ancient titles of Israel (ii. 4—10 ; see
especially his use of the ancient designation of Israel

as a kingly priesthood); and again the conception of various χαρίσματα (iv. 9 f.) to be ministered to all by the several members of the community as stewards of a manifold grace of God. The first four verses of chap. v. must be addressed to 'Elders' in the usual official sense, for they speak of "the flock of God" and of "the chief shepherd," and lay down instructions for the right tending of the flock. But St Peter seems to join with this the original or etymological sense when he calls himself a fellow-elder, apparently as one who could bear personal testimony to the Christ's sufferings, and when (*v.* 5) he bids the younger be subject to the elder. (For a similar combination see Polycarp 5, 6, where νεώτερος comes between deacons and elders.)

Hebrews I shall venture to pass over. The relations of its teaching to our primary subject are complicated by the peculiarity of the position of the Christians of Palestine at the time. No one can miss the indications of a spirit of brotherhood in chap. xiii., or its allusions to rulers of the Ecclesia vaguely called οἱ ἡγούμενοι.

The Apocalypse I must still more reluctantly pass over, or nearly so, from sheer want of time. In i. 6; v. 10, we have the Hebrew form of that phrase of Exodus which St Peter repeated from the LXX. The seven Ecclesiae of Asia met us once before; and we must leave them now without remark. Perhaps the most interesting point in relation to our subject is the vividness and elaboration with which the representation of the new Ecclesia as the true Israel is worked out, especially in chapters vii., xxi. It is especially noteworthy that in chap. vii., if I mistake not, the twelve thousand from every tribe, described as spoken of by the angel, not as seen by John, are identical with the great multitude which his eyes beheld, the actual multitude out of every nation and tribe etc., the members of a now universal Ecclesia.

On St James's last days I should like to have said a little more : but the most essential points respecting him had to be examined in connexion with the Jerusalem conference ; and what remains, though it belongs to the Apostolic age, belongs also to literature outside the New Testament, and so may fitly find a place elsewhere if I should be permitted to lecture on the remaining part of our subject another time.

As regards St John's later writings it must suffice to remind you once more of chapters xiii.—xvii. of the Gospel as on the whole the weightiest and most pregnant body of teaching on the Ecclesia to be found anywhere in the Bible.

Problems of the Second Century and later.

Here I fear we must break off the examination of the several Epistles, this being the last lecture of the course. At the outset I had hoped at least to be able to deal with the chief ecclesiastical problems of the Second Century, with the material of this kind supplied by Clement of Rome and Hermas, the Didache of the Apostles, Ignatius and Polycarp, Justin Martyr and Irenæus (to name only the chief names). I wished especially to shew how much of the controversial differences of later ages on this subject had their root in the actual necessary experience of those early days, and in the natural falling apart of ideas which in the Apostolic writings are combined and complementary to each other. Without some clear thoughts on these matters it is impossible to understand the real significance of the enormous changes which had begun indeed before the end of the Second Century, but which for the most part belong to a later time (for the West the names of Cyprian, Ambrose, and Augustine will be sufficiently representative). I can do no more now than ask you to think of the different lights in which Church membership might naturally present itself, first when Christians were only scattered sojourners in the midst of a suspicious and often hostile population; next, when they had become, though a minority, yet an important and a tolerated minority; then when they were set on a place of vantage by the civil power, and so were increased by hosts of mere timeservers ; and lastly when they had come to constitute practically the whole population, and a Christian world had come into existence. The fundamental perplexing fact throughout was the paradox of a holy Ecclesia consisting in part of men very unholy. In at least three great sectarian movements of the early ages this is an important element, in Montanism, Novatianism, Donatism : but the fundamental thoughts which in this respect governed these movements are to be found in the writings of justly venerated Fathers.

This is all that I can attempt to say now. If I am permitted to lecture in the Michaelmas Term of next year, and no strong reason for preferring another subject intervenes, I shall hope to carry forward the beginning made this term.

Recapitulation.

In the few remaining minutes I should be glad to gather up with extreme brevity some of the leading results at which we seem to have arrived thus far. The greater part of our time has been taken up with what belongs to the early history rather than the early conceptions of the Christian Ecclesia, but, as was to be expected, what the Gospels offered us belongs almost wholly to the region of conceptions.

The one single saying in which our Lord names the new or Christian Ecclesia marks at once its continuity with the Ecclesia of Israel and its newness as His own, the Messiah's, Ecclesia. It marks also its unity. Lastly it marks its being built on Peter and the other eleven, now ascertained to be fit for this function of foundations by the faith in which they had recognised His Messiahship. We saw how the last evening before the Passion, the evening on which began the transition, so to speak, from the Ministry of Christ to the Ministry of His Ecclesia, was one long unfolding of the inner nature of the Ecclesia, by the feast of Holy Communion (as in Matthew, Mark, Luke), and (as in St John) by the symbolic feetwashing, the conversations and discourses which followed (especially the New Commandment, the Vine and the Branches, and the promise of the other Paraclete), and lastly the prayer that the disciples themselves, the representatives of the future Ecclesia of disciples, and all who should believe on Him through their word, may be One; with the assurance that as the Father sent Him into the world, so He Himself sent them into the world; so that their work was not for themselves, but for the saving of mankind. So too for the new members of the Ecclesia of whom we read in the early chapters of Acts the condition of entrance is the same, personal faith leading to personal discipleship, discipleship to a now ascended Lord. And again the life lived is essentially a life of community, in which each felt himself to hold a trust for the good of all. At first the oneness of the Ecclesia is a visible fact due simply to its limitation to the one city of Jerusalem. Presently it enlarges and includes all the Holy Land, becoming ideally conterminous with the Jewish Ecclesia. But at length discipleship on a large scale springs up at Antioch, and so we have a new Ecclesia. By various words and acts the community of purpose and interests between the two Ecclesiae is maintained: but they remain two. Presently the Ecclesia of Antioch, under the guidance of the Holy Spirit speaking through one or more prophets, sets apart Barnabas and Paul and sends them forth beyond Taurus to preach the Gospel. They go first to the Jews of the Dispersion but have at last to turn to the Gentiles. On their way home they recognise or constitute Ecclesiae of their converts in the several cities and choose for them Elders. Thus there is a multiplication of single Ecclesiae. We need not trace the process further. We find St Paul cultivating the friendliest relations between these different bodies, and sometimes in language grouping together those of a single region: but we do not find him establishing or noticing any formal connexion between those of one region or between all generally. He does however work sedulously to counteract the imminent danger of a specially deadly schism, viz. between the Ecclesiae of Judea (as he calls them) and the Ecclesiae of the Gentile world. When the danger of that schism has been averted, he is able to feel that the Ecclesia is indeed One. Finally in Ephesians, and partly Colossians, he does from his Roman habitation not only set forth emphatically the unity of the whole body, but expatiate in mystic language on its spiritual relation to its unseen Head, catching up and carrying on the language of prophets about the ancient Israel as the bride of Jehovah, and suggest that this one Ecclesia, now sealed as one by the creating of the two peoples into one, is God's primary agent in His ever expanding counsels towards mankind.

As regards the mutual relations between its members, these are set forth in many passages which are apt to be read only as belonging to ethics or to individual religion. We are apt to forget (1) that according to the New Testament (and especially Ephesians) the Christian life is the true human life, and that Christians become true men in proportion as they live up to it, (2) that the right relations between the members of the Christian Society or Ecclesia are simply the normal relations which should subsist between members of the human race, and therefore (3) that all the relations of life, being baptised into Christ, become parts and particular modes of Christian membership, and can be rightly acted out only under its conditions, while Christian fellowship further creates a bond, independent of the ordinary family and other such relations, which has a sacredness of its own. Hence the true life of the Ecclesia consists for the most

part in the hourly and daily converse and behaviour
of all its members, in just that element of human
existence, in short, which rarely crystallizes into what
we call events, notable incidents such as find a place
in histories. The Ecclesia as clothed with those high
attributes set forth by St Paul is realised, as it were,
in those monotonous homelinesses of daily living
rather than in administration or business, though it
were business of the highest kind, the formulation
of creeds, or laws, or policies.

While therefore matters belonging to what is called
the organisation of the Ecclesia are undoubtedly an
important part of the subject, it would be a serious
mistake to treat them as the whole. There is indeed
a certain ambiguity in the word 'organisation' as
thus used. Nothing perhaps has been more prominent in our examination of the Ecclesiae of the
Apostolic age than the fact that the Ecclesia itself,
i.e. apparently the sum of all its male adult members, is the primary body, and, it would seem, even
the primary authority. It may be that this state of
things was in some ways a mark of immaturity ; and
that a better and riper organisation must of necessity involve the creation of more special organs of
the community. Still the very origin and fundamental nature of the Ecclesia as a community of
disciples renders it impossible that the principle
should rightly become obsolete. In a word we cannot
properly speak of an organisation of a community

from which the greater part of its members are excluded. The true way, the Apostolic way, of regarding offices or officers in the Ecclesia is to regard them as organs of its corporate life for special purposes: so that the offices of an Ecclesia at any period are only a part of its organisation, unless indeed it unhappily has no other element of organisation.

In the Apostolic age we have seen that the offices instituted in the Ecclesia were the creation of successive experiences and changes of circumstance, involving at the same time a partial adoption first of Jewish precedents by the Ecclesia of Judea, and then apparently of Judean Christian precedents by the Ecclesiae of the Dispersion and the Gentiles. There is no trace in the New Testament that any ordinances on this subject were prescribed by the Lord, or that any such ordinances were set up as permanently binding by the Twelve or by St Paul or by the Ecclesia at large. Their faith in the Holy Spirit and His perpetual guidance was too much of a reality to make that possible.

The Apostles, we have seen, were essentially personal witnesses of the Lord and His Resurrection, bearing witness by acts of beneficent power and by word, the preaching of the kingdom. Round this, their definite function, grew up in process of time an indefinite authority, the natural and right and necessary consequence of their unique position. It

is difficult to think how the early Ecclesia of Judea
could possibly have staggered on without that apostolic authority ; but it came to the Apostles by the
ordinary action of Divine Providence, not (so far as
we can see) by any formal Divine Command. The
government which they thus exercised was a genuine
government, all the more genuine and effectual because it was in modern phrase constitutional: it did
not supersede the responsibility and action of the
Elders or the Ecclesia at large, but called them out.
About the exceptional position of James there will
be a word to say just now.

The Apostles were not in any proper sense officers
of the Ecclesia. The first officers who are definitely
mentioned are the Seven. I need not repeat the
precise purpose of their appointment. It was for a
strictly subordinate and external function, though
men of wisdom and a holy spirit were needed for it.
Of officers in some respects analogous under the
name διάκονοι, ministrants, deacons, we have been
hearing at Ephesus in 1 Tim., and at least in some
sense at Philippi.

But though the Seven of Jerusalem are the first
officers mentioned, we found reason to suspect that
of still earlier date (certainly not much later) were
the Elders. This apparently universal institution, for
administration and in part for teaching, was adopted
by Christians apparently universally. We have distinct evidence for it in the New Testament at Jeru-

salem, in Lycaonia, at Ephesus, in Crete, and probably at Thessalonica: it is mentioned in the Epistles of St James addressed to Jewish Christians of the whole Dispersion, and of St Peter addressed to the Christians of Asia Minor. Of officers higher than Elders we find nothing that points to an institution or system, nothing like the episcopal system of later times. In the New Testament the word ἐπίσκοπος as applied to men, mainly, if not always, is *not* a title, but a description of the Elder's function. On the other hand the monarchical principle, which is the essence of episcopacy receives in the Apostolic age a practical though a limited recognition, not so much in the absolutely exceptional position of St Peter in the early days at Jerusalem, or the equally exceptional position of St Paul throughout the Ecclesiae of his own foundation, as in the position ultimately held by St James at Jerusalem, and also to a limited extent in the temporary functions entrusted by St Paul to Timothy and Titus when he left them behind for a little while to complete arrangements begun by himself at Ephesus and in Crete respectively.

In this as in so many other things is seen the futility of endeavouring to make the Apostolic history into a set of authoritative precedents, to be rigorously copied without regard to time and place, thus turning the Gospel into a second Levitical Code. The Apostolic age is full of embodiments of purposes and principles of the most instructive kind : but the responsibility of choosing the means was left for ever to the Ecclesia itself, and to each Ecclesia, guided by ancient precedent on the one hand and adaptation to present and future needs on the other. The lesson-book of the Ecclesia, and of every Ecclesia, is not a law but a history.

FOUR SERMONS.

A SERMON PREACHED IN THE NAVE OF ELY
CATHEDRAL AT AN ORDINATION SERVICE
ON JUNE 15, 1873.

JOHN xxi. 17—19.

*He saith unto him the third time, Simon, son of Jonas, lovest
thou me? Peter was grieved because he said unto him
the third time, Lovest thou me? And he said unto him,
Lord, thou knowest all things; thou knowest that I love
thee. Jesus saith unto him, Feed my sheep. Verily,
verily, I say unto thee, When thou wast young, thou
girdedst thyself, and walkedst whither thou wouldest: but
when thou shalt be old, thou shalt stretch forth thy
hands, and another shall gird thee, and carry thee
whither thou wouldest not. This spake he, signifying by
what death he should glorify God. And when he had
spoken this, he saith unto him, Follow me.*

EVERY high crisis in our lives is or ought to be to us
the lifting of a veil; perhaps the lifting of many veils.
Our ordinary occupations of mind and body do not
force upon our sight anything beyond that world of

near and familiar circumstance in which we are all
evidently moving. Either some seclusion from the
common life or some rare stirring of our own inner
nature is usually needed to bring within our ken the
great, deeply seated powers which move the world
and which move ourselves. When the crisis has
passed, the exceptional faculty of sight which it
conferred grows dim. But not in vain, not without
God's appointment. If the vision departs leaving us
unchanged, the fault is our own. It was given us for
a little space that it might be converted by the
alchemy of life into imperishable knowledge, the
foundation of an ever tried and ever renewed faith.

This the often repeated experience of our little
individual lives is an imperfect image of God's
manner of unsealing the eyes of the human race
through the Incarnation of His Son. The story of
that single all-sufficient unveiling of the heavenly
kingdom was entrusted to faithful witnesses, that,
cherished in our memories, it may enable us to stretch
our vision beyond the limits of earthly sight. It
gives support and meaning to every glimpse of things
unseen to which in any manner we ourselves attain;
and, by shewing us the Divine order ruling our whole
mixed existence, it enables the daily way of life to
minister to our growth in wisdom.

This purpose of God in our Lord's manifestation
to His disciples comes out with especial force in the
records of the last few weeks of His sojourn on earth.

After the Resurrection He was no longer dwelling habitually within their sight. He appeared to them only on special occasions ; now to one singly, now to various groups. By His appearances and disappearances He trained them through their bodily senses to know the reality of an existence and a presence of which their bodily senses could at most times tell them nothing ; and accustomed them to obtain from the brief moments of higher vision the needed enlightenment for the long spaces when no exceptional endowment was vouchsafed to them. Fear and amazement came upon them when they suddenly found their Lord in the midst of them. But these were not the emotions which it was His chief purpose to awake. The repeated blessing " Peace be to you " is the dominant word of this His latest converse. In heavenly calm, unruffled by any accompanying sight or sound of wonder, He comes and goes and acts and speaks. With the strength of the finished victory over death and sin He anoints them for the life-long contest to which He sends them forth anew. With the rest following on His accomplished work He encompasses the approaching toil and effort of their work for Him. Yet He speaks not as though henceforth removed from participation in their doings. All their days He will still be with them ; no longer indeed Himself subject to the troubles of mortal life, but drawing them all the while to Himself, and keeping them within the tabernacle of His own eternal peace.

The Epilogue to St John's Gospel, as read at
Morning Prayer, has already brought before us in
unusual detail one of these final manifestations of our
Lord to His disciples. That single chapter offers
itself to our hearts as a Divine message concerning
the sacred service upon which we are all now entering,
and the life-long dedication of which it will be for
some of us the beginning. By dwelling now for a
little while on some few heads chosen out of its
manifold instruction, we may be better able in silent
after meditation to embrace its testimony, the last
testimony delivered by Christ's elect evangelist.

Those early appearances of the Lord at Jerusalem,
in which He shewed that He was indeed risen from
the dead, had done their appointed work. The
anxious days spent in the midst of the multitudes
gathered for the Paschal solemnity were all ended.
The disciples had returned to their homes in Galilee
for the weeks which were to pass before the approach
of Pentecost should summon them again to the holy
city. The departure to Galilee had been by a
command received from the Lord Himself, accompanied by a promise that they should see Him there.
At the opening of St John's last narrative we find
seven out of the eleven resuming their work as
fishermen, probably for the first time. We may well
imagine them as just ending their journey in the

evening at the shore of the lake ; and St Peter's rapid announcement " I go a fishing " as guiding them on the instant to a renewal of their old occupation. Thus the hours of darkness and solitude on the water and the fruitless labour would be their first experience of the new time.

As day dawned, they found that they were not indeed alone. The increasing light revealed to them One standing near on the beach. We all remember the question, the answer, the counsel, the.'laden net ', the recognition by St John followed by St Peter's hasty wading to the shore while the other disciples continued the labour to which the Lord had given success.

The second part of the narrative introduces a fresh miracle and a fresh lesson. Immediately on landing, the disciples behold not only a fire already lighted, but a fish already laid thereon and bread. Jesus bids them bring of the produce of their haul. Rejoicing to obey a personal command, St Peter hastens to drag the net up on the land to the Lord's feet ; and none of the living spoil is lost. Yet the disciples' draught was not to be for their own use. Jesus invites them as a host invites his guests, that they may break their fast after the toilsome night with the fish and the bread of His providing. As He prospered their toil, so also He gives from His own hand the food which is to restore their strength.

Then it was, while the awe and the joy were still

new, that Christ turned to the disciple whose true zeal
had borne some marks of self-will and self-assertion,
with the searching question, "Simon, son of John,
lovest thou me more than these?" Was Peter
cherishing a thought that, because he had hurried
from his work and his brethren to enjoy his Master's
presence, he must needs love Him more than they
did? Had he forgotten that promise of exceeding
fidelity, of which the sequel had been the thrice
repeated denial? His love might possibly be in some
sense greater than theirs, and yet it might be less
precious to the perfect Lord, because less ripened by
self-conquest from a natural impulse into a far-sighted
devotion of spirit.

The humbling hours of the Passion had not left .
Peter unchanged. He dared not claim pre-eminence
in affection, but standing as it were alone before his
Lord, he could fearlessly say that he did indeed hold
his Master dear. The reply reminded him why he
had been called into that intimacy of personal relation. It was not that he might enjoy for himself the
felicity of being close to the tenderest of friends and
most merciful of saviours, nor even that he might be
able to cultivate in himself all heavenly graces by
means of that hallowing intercourse. It was .that he
might render faithful service to a Divine Shepherd by
rendering faithful service to His flock.

Two different kinds of service to the flock are
hidden behind the one word "feed". The first and

the last of the three commands speak of "feeding" the lambs or the sheep in the strict sense: they enjoin that care which consists in the providing fit pasture. The second time St Peter is bidden rather to tend the sheep, to exercise that care of them of which the shepherd's rod and staff in the twenty-third Psalm are the symbols, the care of government and guidance. Thus while the Lord disowns that devotion to Himself which does not include devotion to the needs of His people, He suggests the varied gifts in ever changing use which are required for its exercise, the patient love and studious solicitude presupposed by a service having such ends in view. But it is His own person, words, and acts that supply the ruling standard under which all this pastoral language has to be brought and without which it becomes little more than casual imagery. He who speaks is the Shepherd of shepherds, the Good Shepherd, newly risen from the grave into which He had been brought by laying down His life to the uttermost for His sheep. The feeding and governing of the sheep are but parts of that wonder-working sacrifice; when any other spirit reigns in them, they fall away from the love of Christ.

Thus the commands which Christ lays on His apostle, in reply to the proffered love, are in no sense a slighting of personal bonds in comparison of official duties. They are a warning alike against sinking the man in the apostle or the apostle in the man. With-

out a pause' Christ goes on from the charge to feed
His sheep to words that tell only of God's dealings
with the individual life: "Verily, verily, I say unto
thee, when thou wast younger, thou girdedst thyself
and walkedst whither thou wouldest: but when thou
shalt be old, thou shalt stretch out thy hands and
another shall gird thee and bear thee where thou
wouldest not." The words in part describe the
natural course of age as it comes upon every man
who reaches the full term of years. On the beginning
of manhood are bestowed free choice and spontaneous
movement. The fetters which the world without and
decay within are thenceforth without ceasing forging
in secret, must at length tighten their pressure as the
last passive and helpless stage draws on. But in
St Peter's case this natural bondage to circumstance
had already put on a higher form. Already he had
used the freedom of his manhood to give himself over
to a Divine master. From the hour when he first
forsook his nets to follow Jesus, he had surrendered
the youthful power of choosing to what tasks he
should gird himself and of going whither he would.
Nay, as he went forward in his chosen course, he
could not but rouse against himself a host of gainsayers and enemies. A violent death like his Lord's
should crown a life of restraint.

These were not words of doom : they were part of
an approving consecration. It had not been in vain-
glorious self-confidence that Peter had called on the

all-knowing Lord to read his heart: because he did love Him, therefore it was that he was worthy to feed and guide His sheep. Then followed the setting of the seal. "When he had thus spoken, he saith unto him, Follow me." The two words summoned up for St Peter the life of all his past from the day when his brother Andrew had come to him and said, "We have found the Messiah", and that other day beside the lake when the nets were forsaken. Discipleship in those its earliest beginnings was shut up in the two words, and the outward act which they denoted. Since that time the whole Ministry of word and deed had intervened, and then the Passion and Death, and then the Resurrection. But now, after all his added experiences concerning Christ and concerning himself, the same words remained the truest. A new world of meaning had unfolded itself in the idea of following Christ, and yet more in his knowledge of Christ's own Person and Nature. With the warning prophecy ringing in his ears, and the recollections of the last days at Jerusalem thronging his heart, the command came upon him with an unearthly solemnity. But it came also with the unearthly peace of assured forgiveness and the unearthly hope of a high and ever higher calling.

Today we listen with hushed and abashed hearts to the mysterious colloquy between the Lord and the

Apostle. We cannot but be aware how much of its meaning is still obscure to us : but to our consciences it finds its way with a piercing clearness. We shall soon hear it repeated to us in other language in the forms by which the Church admits new members into her undying apostolate. The commission now to be given looks back to an earlier probation, and a yet earlier call. In all cases in which the acceptance of the holy commission has not been a grievous profanation, there has been beforehand some drawing towards the presence and service of Christ ; sometimes perhaps dating only from later days, but oftener to be traced back to the aspirations which spring from a pure and devout home. This unripened love of Christ has perhaps suffered much in the first years of manhood ; has been chilled, stunted, forgotten, dishonoured, even denied. Yet now it has renewed its growth once more, and desires to be accepted and employed. Whoever offers himself, as here today, must have already heard Christ saying to him, " Lovest thou me ? " and must have already dared to say, knowing that he is uttering the innermost desire of his heart, Yea, Lord, thou knowest that I love thee.

Then follows the charge itself. It is first an acceptance of the offered love. It is then the reward of the offered love by the gift of appropriate service to be rendered. It is a prohibition of that delusive counterfeit of love which refuses to see Christ in all whom He died to redeem. It opens to love a boundless future by linking it to an inexhaustible world of duty.

Yet with these life-giving promises there is mingled the unfaltering sentence of restraint and tribulation. They who deliberately take upon them vows like these must surely have counted well the cost. They must have searched well and found in themselves firm readiness not merely to take up joyfully the labours and responsibilities of their work, but to embrace loss of pleasures, loss of gains, undeserved shames, and mortifications, it may be (in the lawless times to come) yet worse injuries, as the natural accompaniments of true and faithful service. The season of self-girding is doomed to pass quickly away.

When this stern condition of heavenly ministry upon earth has been heard and accepted, the voice of the Chief Shepherd lifts up all hearts once more with the single summons, Follow me. Now we know of a truth what it is to follow Him, because we have learned to know Himself, and the purposes of His work, and the means by which He brings them to pass. And thus we can treasure the summons in our memories, and humbly bow down our heads to receive power from on high.

And so when we go forth to execute Christ's Ministry, we shall learn to measure the range and requirements of our office by nothing less than the standard of His own infinite dealings with man. On the one hand we shall learn to neglect whatever cannot be used for the feeding or the guiding of His sheep; while on the other hand we shall discover how varied a world of action is contained within those twin functions when they are rightly understood in their full breadth, what manifold materials for building up towards Divine ends we may find both within ourselves and strewed around us, and what unwearied advances in wisdom and charity we shall need to be able to employ them aright. We shall remember that the whole nature of those committed to our charge is worthy of being brought to perfection in Christ, and therefore has a claim on us for such food for mind and spirit as we can supply. We shall not shrink from the heavy responsibility of guidance and government, as the first conditions of Christian society, and the best safeguards of unity and freedom; but we shall know that they are difficult and anxious tasks laid upon us for the welfare of the flock, not privileges to be enjoyed in the ignoble lust of domination.

We turn once more to ourselves; but in so doing we do not turn away from our work. This is the prerogative of the Christian ministry, that it coincides with the highest form of personal life, embracing as it does the whole range of our nature, and working towards unity and perfection through communion with our Divine Head. To feed and tend Christ's sheep and to follow Him are but different sides of the same life-long striving. We feel that this is indeed their true relation, when following St John's guidance we look onward beyond ourselves, beyond Christ's flock, beyond Christ Himself to that which was the ultimate end of His own work for man's salvation, even the Glory of God.

Today it is easy to keep thoughts like these in mind. After a while there is danger that they may come to seem unreal. The brutishness or triviality in which millions around us pass their lives, and perhaps the chilling inroads of professional routine in our own work, not to speak of sadder and deeper causes, may render it hard for us to rule or judge the petty doings of each day by the words which Christ spoke to His Apostle. The veil which is now drawn asunder may close over us again. If so it should be, let us think of the disciples at their unprofitable toil on the water. Let us mark the slow recognition of the Lord standing on the firm land beyond the water, the completed work, the partaking of His food. Let us bathe His words afresh in the dewy brightness of the early summer morning by the Galilean lake. So we may come to know the power of the new life of which that peaceful brightness was the sacrament, the new life that dawned on mankind when God raised His Son from the dead.

A SERMON PREACHED AT THE UNIVERSITY COMMEMORATION OF BENEFACTORS, OCT. 31, 1875.

PSALM cxlix. 2 (part).

Let Israel rejoice in him that made him.

WE are met today for a twofold service of praise; the praise of God and the praise of men. Such has been the clear and ample teaching of the consecrated words appointed for our guidance. In the praise of God all the varying strains of the Psalter meet together, and we have begun our worship[1] with singing the last three of those closing hymns of the Psalter which set forth the praise of God in one unbroken strain. On the other hand we have next listened[2] to the opening verses of that Hymn of the Fathers, as an ancient title calls it, which bids us now praise famous men and our fathers that begat us, and declares that the

---

[1] The special Psalms appointed for the University Commemoration of Benefactors are Ps. cxlviii. Ps. cxlix. Ps. cl.

[2] The special Lesson is Ecclesiasticus xliv. 1—15.

people will tell of their wisdom, and the congregation will shew forth their praise. Both praises rested on the same foundation, and the one led to the other. The Hallelujah Psalms came forth after long centuries of trial and vicissitude : they are the voice of chastened and restored Israel looking back over the mighty works of Jehovah wrought through patriarchs, chieftains, kings, and prophets. It is under the inspiration of these Psalms, and others like them, that the son of Sirach[1] lifts up the praises of famous men, the fathers of Israel. First he speaks in such words as these : " Though we say many things, we shall never attain ; and the end of words is, He is the whole " (Ecclus. xliii. 27). " Who hath seen Him, and shall declare it ? and who shall magnify Him as He is ? Many things yet hidden are greater than these, for we have seen but a few of His works. For all things were made by the Lord, and to the godly gave He wisdom " (xliii. 31 ff.). Then he exalts the supreme praise by joining it with the memory of Enoch, Noah, Moses, and the rest, ending with Simon the High Priest, men permitted to have a share in God's work of making Israel, and endowed with the wisdom which springs from fearing His holy name.

Even so is it always. By love and thankfulness and reverence towards human parents and teachers we first learn what it is to worship God ; and the lesson is quickly either unlearned or falsified as soon

[1] See Ecclesiasticus xliii. 27, 32 ; xlv. 16—l. 24.

as we strive to banish all lower homages that He may be adored alone. With the growing perception of fresh subordinate objects for thankful praise grows also the power to praise Him according to His excellent greatness ; and in the welcoming of these many rights over our hearts His praise is sustained and fulfilled. Not the least of the blessings conferred by enlargement of knowledge is the discovery of hidden companies of benefactors in the teeming past. According as the circles of immediate time or neighbourhood are overpassed, and we gain some true sense of the various great societies into some of which we are all born or early incorporated, and then of the deep debts which the present life of each society owes to far reaching lines of wise counsels and great deeds in bygone days, all history becomes to us full of occasions for a purifying and invigorating joy, by reason of its multiplied demands on our gratitude to elder brethren of old. And the multiplied homage thus awakened, just and reasonable and helpful though it be known to be, is found fugitive and unsatisfying unless it is blended into a deeper praise of the one King of the ages, by whose counsel the ministries of each generation are appointed and marshalled for that future towards which we too have the privilege of bending our lives.

It is in the ancestries of a Church or a nation, to say nothing of the larger ancestries of the Church

Universal or of mankind, that the blessing of the two-fold praise is best discerned. Yet it is provided for us in ample measure in the history of that lesser society which it is our pride here to serve. Today's worship invites us to take to ourselves the blessing, and through it to seek light and strength for the tasks of the coming year and the coming age. There is no danger now of being estranged from present realities by looking dutifully and gratefully back to whatever we can find worthy of admiration in our long annals. Rather shall we so be enabled in some measure to rise above the pettinesses and blindnesses which absorbing work creates as much as it dispels, and to obtain some impulse and guidance towards such wide and high purposes as can alone confer the power either of perceiving our true duties or of accomplishing them. The true enemy of the future is not the past but the tyrannous present, often usurping the semblance of the past to disguise its own oppressions. It is possible for either the love of the past or the love of the future to exist apart : but it is not possible for either to accomplish beneficent and lasting results without the other.

The names to be recited today represent directly one kind of benefits, chiefly the gifts of property by which institutions of various kinds essential to our work have been founded or maintained. Among these names occur not a few belonging likewise to another class of benefactors whose memory we cannot

but yet more dutifully cherish, members of our own
body and therefore forefathers in a stricter sense, who
gave to the University or its studies the gift of their
own lives and energies.   Other names we shall hear
of men who went forth from among us in manhood
to various callings in life; but though long removed
from any of the enchantments which might be
thought to invest the University with an illusive
glory to the eyes of those who make it their home,
could yet after their fullest experience find no way
so sure for bestowing their bounty for the public
good as by strengthening or enlarging the resources
of University study.   The remaining names belong
to benefactors who never lived within our walls, and
therefore were bound to us by no filial tie, yet recognised from a distance the almost hidden source of
powers indispensable to the life of the commonwealth.   With these let us join in thought the founders
of our Colleges, not formally commemorated here,
doubtless because specially commemorated in their
several Houses, but worthy of being remembered
among the foremost when we pass in review the
obligations of the University itself to earlier ages.
They have a peculiar claim to be remembered now
because their gifts are the memorials of successive
restorative reforms carried on at no long intervals
through more than three hundred years, in the midst
of which the Revival of Letters and the Reformation
appear only as episodes, and the continuous life of

the University reflects the continuous life of the nation from the days of the first Edward to those of Elizabeth.

Once more, if we may rightly count among benefactors those to whom the removal of abuses and the introduction of improvements and expansions of administration is mainly due, there are many in the last three or four generations nearest to our own times whom it would be base indeed to put out of remembrance just now. When we hear the University extolled for awaking out of slumber to a tardy sense of neglected duty, we may think it vain to attempt to appreciate the worth of either the reproof or the praise so far as it affects ourselves. But we cannot forget that from a time long before any of us were born the University and its Colleges have been going silently and steadily onward, often perfecting existing work, often entering on new fields of work: and further we know that this progress has been set forward and guided entirely from within, first commended and laboured for by far-sighted rulers or leaders, and then sooner or later obtaining from others the needful amount of consent. The praise belongs not to us but to our fathers who begat us, and yet more to Him who has granted to us not only the heritage of long ages but the privilege and help of walking in the footsteps of men who in their day approved themselves worthy heirs.

It remains for us, brethren, by God's grace to work out our thanksgiving to its rightful fruits. The offering of praise has no meaning except as the offering of ready and willing hearts. Every thanksgiving rendered to our fellow men, whether living or dead, is an acknowledgement that we are appointed to be links in a spiritual chain of transmitted blessing, bound and glorified by the fundamental law of possession under the Gospel, Freely ye have received, freely give. Every thanksgiving to God is an acknowledgement of a bestowed capacity for higher or more effectual service.

It cannot then be unfitting to join with our present thanksgivings of today some thoughts on the office which seems traced out for our society, partly by our own history, partly by the actual wants of English society at large. Not a few of the matters which are now constantly discussed among us, intermingling with the round of necessary employments, must ultimately be ruled by principles of which it is seasonable to speak in the House of God, most of all in this House of God which was for so long the place of meeting for our ancient assembly. Neither on this subject nor on any other is it possible that all the beliefs expressed here should find universal assent among us. But if, as is surely true, our main differences of view respecting academic policy resolve themselves into different assignments of proportional value to objects all recognised as good, we may justly hope to be led on the way to more complete harmony by bringing our counsels into the presence of Him whose Lordship governs into unity all several agencies within each society, and all several societies within His universal family ; Him to whose making and remaking we, like Israel, must at last refer, whatever as time goes on we may be enabled to be.

The popular voice commends us for beginning to render the University more national than heretofore. All our habits teach us to distrust a sonorous word until it has been studied and tried ; but they do not forbid us to accept the study and trial of it as belonging to our immediate duty. We should certainly have no right to leave our forefathers under the imputation of having a less national spirit than ourselves because the recipients of their direct teaching did not for the most part belong to the classes forming the larger proportion of the nation. It would be helping to keep alive a dangerous delusion to speak as if all members of the body had the same office, and the member which duly discharged its own office were not thereby ministering to the rest. So far as any particular classes received from the University qualifications to do the work required of them on behalf of the whole, the service which it rendered to them was in fact rendered to the whole. Unless we hold firmly this the Christian conception of a body politic, and rule ourselves consistently by it now and always, we shall but condemn ourselves and our University to poor and trivial uses, blind leaders of the blind, as well as unjust and undutiful descendants of those to whose place we have succeeded.

But when we have taken this principle to guide us, we shall not find ourselves thereby absolved from the responsibility of considering how far applications of it which were tolerably adequate once will suffice under changed circumstances. It is not enough to maintain that we are discharging a national function in the truest sense : we are bound to go on to enquire whether other functions remain for which we have the requisite capacity without abandoning our present employments, and which it would be for the advantage of the nation that we should undertake. If such should prove to be the case, we cannot limit the standard of duty by the sufficiencies of a former state of things.

At the outset we are compelled to remember that it is chiefly action of our own that has given birth to the comments which we feel to be half untrue. It is because we have already for years past been leaving behind us the old boundaries that we are coming to be estimated not so much by the appropriateness or value of our work as by its breadth of visible distribution. Wants have been gradually perceived which we have been glad to attempt to supply. Examinations cautiously extended have enabled us to help in elevating and directing a vast amount of teaching in which it was impossible for us to take any other part.

Members of our body have lately carried personal teaching in the name of the University into centres of dense population. Few among us will regret these steps, and yet it is no wonder they suggest to beholders that the goal towards which we are moving is that equalised and diffused utility which is assumed to be the test of a national spirit.

But if these recent extensions of labour are easily misinterpreted, they are at the same time modes of fulfilling an office which may justly be called national. In so far as they lead all classes to see in the University a common friend and guide, the bestower of valued instruction and knowledge, the University becomes a bond between class and class, such as old bitternesses render it unhappily vain to seek elsewhere just now. Before personal contact many alienations melt away which would otherwise aggravate the deadliest diseases of the commonwealth. But above all, if only the University remains true to its proudest boast of upholding at all costs the supreme worth of liberal education, and perseveringly translates the significant watchword into varying applications according to the circumstances of various classes, it is thereby strengthening and consolidating every good influence already at work. To supply fresh weapons for strife, or even fresh means for subsistence, is no part of its vocation : in purchasing favour by such gifts as these, it would cast away its proper beneficent virtue. By presenting knowledge as none of these

17—2

things,—nor yet as a luxury for the idle, which may be prudently let alone till all other cravings are satisfied, but as then most to be prized for its own sake when it has to compete with the cares and conflicts of life, the University at once proclaims its own unvarying characteristic, and becomes a potent restorer of social order.

These considerations will amply justify us in regarding the University as charged with the responsibilities of a fresh national office by virtue of its widened operations, however strongly we may feel the unsoundness of the grounds on which others arrive at what wears the appearance of being the same result. There are however different and even graver national responsibilities which though not new, have now a rapidly increasing claim to be embraced, and for the discharge of which we cannot too anxiously provide in all present and future arrangements. Perhaps our greatest danger now is of frittering away force in too various activity, and suffering external work to sap that energy of progressive study within our own precincts which is for our purposes the very breath of life. Thus the farther we enlarge the outer and remoter borders of our domain, the greater the need to concentrate the resources for the cultivation of the higher departments of knowledge here in the midst. The inherited employment of educating certain limited classes, the members of which are destined in due time to stand where the effects of their nurture for good or ill will deeply affect all classes around them, has lost none of its old value ; and we are rightly glad to add to their number from the best representatives of other classes. But this employment would lose none of its usefulness if it were associated with an influence felt by the adult and scattered members of the educated classes elsewhere no less than by those who are passing in youth through a University course.

If it is a pernicious error to treat liberal knowledge as a luxury for the citizen, still less, at whatever cost of seeming to magnify our office in delusive conceit, dare we speak or act as though a metropolis of liberal knowledge were a luxury for the nation. In some states of society the ethical and properly spiritual forces may suffice to resist dissolution ; but with the spread of loose and unsifted promiscuous knowledge they cannot long hold their ground alone on the large scale. It would be difficult to over-estimate the auxiliary remedial virtue of calm and mature knowledge, vivified by careful and independent thought, except when it is unnaturally divorced from a high ethical standard. In the University as its natural home such salutary knowledge should grow freely and abundantly, not maintaining a difficult existence among surrounding hindrances, as when it springs up sporadically elsewhere, but fostered and nourished by the dominant influences of the place. Where the ascertainment, the preservation, and the communication of truth are made the primary business of life by a varied society of men, regulated and united by the performance of known duties, a better ideal and a sounder exercise of knowledge would assuredly arise. The evils which spring from partial and disproportionate knowledge would be neutralised by the mutual correction and combination of the various provinces of knowledge ; and though such a society, like every society devoted chiefly to a single purpose, would be liable to perils of its own, this is but the universal condition of a finite world where all things are done by part and part. Nor would it be a small safeguard that the office of teaching must as a rule be jealously retained and enforced as heretofore, for reasons not needing comment here. Not exemption from sometimes unwelcome labour is to be desired for members of an English University, but freedom to pursue a student's life from stage to stage, and to die humble learners.

Doubtless the true nature and use of such an institution would never be widely understood or valued. It has been well said that it belongs to a University to be the refuge for unpopular doctrines, the storehouse where truths long said to have been exploded are preserved from oblivion till their hour comes round again once more. This is in other words to claim for a University the high privilege of escaping subjection to each surging wave of opinion as it hides the ocean before it follows its predecessor out of sight, of welcoming the truth and right in each of two or more contending sides, and of maintaining by preference that cause, which finds fewest spokesmen in the world without. The description may at least be accepted as applicable to a University in proportion as it takes its stand on truth and the harmony of truth ; and surely it is needless to urge how opportune a corrective to recklessness and faction such a capacity and temper might supply. Nor is there any real danger in this age of the world lest seclusion should breed estrangement from current thoughts and ways. The danger lies rather in the other direction, in the morbid fear of being branded as pedants if we do not mimic the tones prevailing in circles of society which are inspired by altogether different principles. Fidelity to a special function is always a primary duty ; while on the other hand the function of a University imperatively demands that its members should take vigilant note of the leading phases of movement around them, as foremost materials for dispassionate examination ; unable perhaps to join in any popular cry, but ready to find instruction in all.

On that which is perhaps the greatest question of all, the relation of the University to the Church and to all that the Church represents, it is better to say nothing today than such few and insufficient words as would alone be possible now.   In this time of distrust and separation, when diversities of work are eagerly embittered into oppositions of nature, God has granted peace to our Israel.   Be it our care that it bring forth the Divine fruits of peace to the glory of His holy Name.

We have been led this morning to think much of the lofty ends which our University may perhaps in due time be called to fulfil.   It does not seem too rash a hope, when we think on the past which we commemorate in this service of praise, the latent powers which we find not to have wholly departed from among us, the open field of an ancient nation reawakening to the thirst for knowledge.   We know that the past was not all glorious.   We know better still our own weaknesses, follies, sins.   When we think of them, it seems as though we were fated to disappoint any hopes that we might cherish for our society.   Yet He in whose hands the future lies is with us still.   In the power of the Gospel of His eternal Son we learn even through humiliation to rejoice in Him that made us, and to trust that through humiliation still, if in no other way, He will make us always even to the end.

THE GROWTH OF A COLLEGE INTO A TEMPLE IN THE UNIVERSAL TEMPLE.

A SERMON PREACHED IN EMMANUEL COLLEGE CHAPEL, CAMBRIDGE, ON FEB. 24, 1889.

EPHESIANS iv. 4.

One Body. *One Spirit.*

EPHESIANS ii. 21.

In whom each several building, fitly framed together, groweth into a holy temple in the Lord.

THESE words meet our eyes every time that we enter this chapel. Their first or immediate purpose as they stand there is to set forth in consecrated language the guiding principles on which the windows and walls of the chapel have been peopled with the forms and names of men of other generations[1]; to set us on the right way for following the arrangement of the various parts which make up the whole; and to suggest to us the thoughts through which they become far more than adornments or curiosities. The words are no mere key to the details of a material

[1] See Appendix.

fabric. They point rather to that invisible structure of living stones which gathers beneath its roof, holding up to us the highest aspect of the purposes for which our College itself exists. They press upon us the thought of its relation to God's whole purpose concerning mankind. What the texts teach as eternal and unchanging truth is echoed back and exemplified by the message of the walls and windows, by which the College is visibly linked to the spiritual history of Christendom.

It will be worth our while this morning to consider these pregnant words of Scripture in this their application to the lessons of the building in which we meet together for worship. I do not propose to speak singly of the lives or works of the forty men of other days who for one reason or another are commemorated here, full of interest as the recital would in most cases be. We shall have enough to occupy us in tracing out the fundamental teachings which they together suggest to us, and by which they speak to us for our help and guidance in the difficulties and duties of our own day.

Many of us perhaps will be glad to be reminded of the general plan on which the memorial adornments of the chapel have been arranged. The two western pairs of windows and the western pair of panels are devoted to the commemoration of illustrious sons of the College itself. The two eastern pairs of both windows and panels carry back the spiritual ancestry of the College to early Christian days. Within the narrow limits of our space a few only can find room out of a great host. These few are the chosen representatives of chosen periods out of the long line of centuries. They were men of the most various characters compatible with singleness of Christian purpose, moulded by the most various circumstances, thinking the most various thoughts and speaking the most various words. In their united voice we hear echoed the endless manifoldness of the one comprehensive truth; and with scarcely any exceptions they have all this characteristic that they were men consciously on a forward march, zealous for new good, labourers in the cause of a better future.

A thousand years of Christian faith are spanned in the two eastern windows. The Fathers, as they are called, of Christian theology have for their spokesmen two men of rare goodness and rare genius, who have at different times exercised a singular power in moulding the thoughts of other ages on the highest subjects, a power far from being exhausted yet, Origen the Alexandrian Greek of the third century, and Augustine the Carthaginian Latin of the fifth century. These are men of the old world. Beside them in the same windows stand precursors of the new world; John the monk from Ireland, who revived the deeper thoughts of ancient Greek theology; and Anselm the righteous Archbishop, from whom the Latin theology of the Middle Ages chiefly took its rise.

The next pair of windows sets before us that great change not in the theology only, but in the whole life, of Northern Europe which we call the Reformation of the 16th Century, an event which must have a peculiar interest for ourselves because it led to the foundation of our College. The age of the English Reformation is represented to us by four wholly different men, two of whom were early workers on behalf of practical reforms, while they left the existing framework of belief and Church politics unquestioned ; and the other two were active leaders in the Reformation itself. Beside Colet with his grave Christian humanism, and Fisher with his zeal for the restoration and propagation of learning, stand Tyndale, one of the many simple students whose hearts were kindled by the new fire, holding our first printed English New Testament, which he bequeathed to us with his blood ; and Cranmer the statesman prelate, whose best monument is the First English Prayer-book, a true symbol of all the better elements in his tragically mixed career. The witness of the last three of these four was consummated at last in that highest form of witness which can be held up to a luxurious and easy-going age : they laid down their lives for conscience sake : they received the martyr's crown.

Thus far we have been gathering up some of the teaching of the two eastern pairs of windows : the panels have likewise a story of their own to tell. The two Elizabethan Colleges, of which Emmanuel was the earlier, were built on the site and even on the ruins of the convents belonging to the two great orders of friars, that is, 'brethren', who had gone forth from Southern Europe early in the 13th century to be in different ways the messengers of a more energetic and popular form of religious life through Western Christendom. Between that time and the Reformation these two orders had for the most part fallen away from their early greatness: but meanwhile they had been able to count among their members no small proportion of the most illustrious theologians and philosophers of the Middle Ages. With good reason therefore are our easternmost panels inscribed with the names of Dominic, founder of the Preaching Friars or Dominicans, to whose home in Cambridge we of this College have succeeded; and of Francis of Assisi, founder of the Friars Minor or Franciscans; and with the names of a chosen few out of each order, ending in each case with the name of one who was in some manner an unconscious herald of the coming Reformation.

But the renewal of life and light by the Reformation is not the only great renewal with which God in His manifold goodness has blessed the churches and peoples of Europe in these later centuries. Step by step He has opened to us two wide universes of knowledge, the knowledge of man and the knowledge of nature, for the progressive education and enrichment of the human race, and not least for its better knowledge of Himself and His dealings with His creatures. In our middle panels are commemorated some of the great pioneers in the restoration or establishment of knowledge in these two wide worlds. On the South stand the names of some of those who in the central culmination and the late decay of the Middle Ages, from Dante onwards, contributed most to that growing expansion of the human mind and spirit which took definite shape in a new knowledge of all that is written in the literature and art of other generations. The opposite panel on the North side is a record of that upgrowth of disciplined study and imagination which has given us the ever deepening knowledge of nature ; commemorating the two chief prophets of its early growth, and two illustrious representatives of its achievements in the organic and the inorganic realms.

In the remaining windows and panels we learn to cherish the memory of some of those members of our College who, by their aspirations and words and deeds for their own day, have shown themselves worthy heirs of the great heritage of the past. They illustrate three great waves of religious movement which passed over England during the first 100 years of the existence of the College, each governed by a limited or onesided view of truth, yet all contributing to its perfect sum. First, as many know, came that strenuous and compact system of belief and practice which was first worked out at Geneva, an attempt to organise Christian faith and Christian life entirely

anew on the basis of the letter of the Old and New
Testaments without regard to history or to existing
institutions. After a while there arose, preeminently
within our own walls, a generation of men to whom
the rigid barriers erected by the elder school were an
offence ; men who rejoiced to recognise traces of
God's light and God's love far and wide among
mankind, and read the universe afresh by the spirit
of Divine sonship, but who hardly faced the more
complex problems of Christian thought, or took
account of the needs and conditions of fellowship in
the Christian body. And then, thirdly, came the men
of the Restoration, less directly entrusted than their
predecessors of either school with the championship
of a new message of truth or life, but moved by a
strong reaction against the negative and destructive
elements in the religious policy of the Commonwealth,
and a natural zeal and affection for ancient institutions and customs which had for the time been sup-
pressed. Among our Emmanuel worthies all these
movements have fit representatives ; while some of
the number are yet more worthy to be remembered
for their own lives or writings.

Thus far we have been proceeding from East to
West. But, through at least the whole course of the
windows, the North and South sides have for the
most part each a character of its own. It would be
scarcely wrong, borrowing the ancient Greek antithesis, to say that on the North are chiefly ranged the

men of action, on the South the men of contemplation.   The men on the North were mainly illustrious
in government or other direct and visible service
rendered to their brethren : in theology, their common
characteristic was a love of form and definiteness.
The men on the South were mainly students, whose
work was done by the written or spoken word or
by personal influence ; and who as theologians, in
their search for ultimate principles, feared not to
explore reverently the more mysterious regions of
thought, at the risk of being called mystics, or suffering worse reproaches from those who preferred to
walk only in beaten ways.

If now, leaving the sides of the chapel, we turn to
the East end, where each of the two lines meets an
independent justification in an apostolic sentence
below, we shall see that they end above in a double
form of apostolic words, in which they find their
mutual harmony and mutual necessity.   We read
there *One Body, One Spirit:* and those who look
down upon us from the northern windows have
earned our veneration preeminently by their service
to the Body of Christ, and they of the southern
windows preeminently by their service to the Spirit
of Christ.

One Body, One Spirit.   Each implies the other.
In the religious life of men the Bible knows nothing
of a Spirit floating, as it were, detached and un-
clothed.   The operation of the Spirit is in the life

and harmony of the parts and particles of the body in which, so to speak, it resides. And conversely a society of men deserves the name of a body in the Scriptural sense in proportion as it becomes a perfect vehicle and instrument of the Spirit.

What then is this One Body, *unum corpus*, ἓν σῶμα? It is possible that, taken in their context, these two words refer first to the local body formed of those Christians to whom the Epistle was addressed. But at least they derive their ultimate force from a reference, tacit if it be not express, to the one universal Body and the one universal Spirit of which St Paul speaks elsewhere. That body is, I need hardly say, the Universal Church made up of men in great part divided from each other by all sorts of earthly conditions, but united by the confession of the One Lord, which unfolds itself into the one faith, and is sealed and consecrated by the one baptism; appointed to be the representatives of God and His presence to mankind, the leaven which is to work till all humanity is leavened. This comprehensive society is described by the image of a body with reference to two equally vital truths; the mutual need and mutual service of the individual Christians who are its members; and the dependence of each and all for unity and life and all things on Him who is in St Paul's language the Head. "For as the body is one," he writes to the Corinthians (1 Cor. xii. 12 ff.), "and hath many members, and· all the members of

H. E.   18

the body, being many, are one body, so also is Christ. For in one Spirit were we all baptised into one body, whether Jews or Greeks, whether bond or free; and were all made to drink of one Spirit. For the body is not one member, but many."

But while St Paul thus raises our thoughts to the contemplation of that universal Body which now stretches through so many centuries and among such countless races, he at the same time brings its religious import very close to us in the narrow circles of our own surroundings. " In Christ Jesus," he told the Ephesians, "each several building fitly framed together groweth into a holy temple in the Lord; in whom ye also are builded together for a habitation of God in the Spirit."

We must pause for a moment to observe that the image here is changed. We seem to hear now not of a body but of a building. But elsewhere in the Epistle the two images are carefully interwoven one with another :—"unto the building up of the body of Christ" (iv. 12): "maketh the increase of the body unto the building up of itself in love" (iv. 16). So also by a bold paradox St Peter makes mention of "living stones built up into a spiritual house." The image of the body speaks to us of life, movement, growth, feeling, diversity of functions: the image of the building speaks to us of permanence, of foundation and superstructure, of the fitting and compacting of sharply individual units, but most of all of habitation ; the universal body formed of Christian men, not a stone fabric built by human hands, being according to the New Testament the true dwelling place of God on earth.

But what should specially be noticed in the text which we are now considering is that the truth taught by St Paul with reference to the highest sphere is a principle of universal application for every society, great or small, which with others goes to make up the supreme society. Each several building formed by the gathering together of Christians into one society shares all the privileges of the one all-comprehending building or body. Its unity and its strength come from the invisible Lord in the heavens who holds it together : in fulfilling its own limited purpose it becomes a holy temple in the midst of which, to use the figurative language which alone is possible on such high themes, God Himself makes His abode.

It is wholly therefore within the spirit of St Paul's meaning to apply his words to that little local society of which we now present are members. Assuredly our life here, with all its work and all its intercourse, will be sound and bright, rich in present and in future good, in proportion as we look on the College of living men as a body made one by heavenly bonds, an invisible fabric, the shrine of a Divine presence.

The thought is doubtless a difficult one. Yet surely we have great helps towards grasping it afforded us by the windows and walls of this chapel, the place where we meet as members of a body, and join in worship founded on the recognition of Jesus Christ as the Head of His Church. Those forms and names which represent to us the first fifteen Christian centuries, however scanty their number, do in some sort set before us, first, the great universal society which St Paul beheld in its infancy; and then that portion of it which has the highest claims on us as Englishmen, our own national Church in the days of the Reformation. Nor, in passing from the one to the other, need we so misinterpret the necessary narrowing of scope as to forget our fellowship, then and now, with the Christians and the Churches of other lands. A second narrowing meets us, a narrowing to a far smaller Christian society, when we go on in mind to that part of the Chapel in which our own brethren of Emmanuel are commemorated. The College, we all I hope know, was founded only about a generation after the close of that former stormy time; and the purpose of it was to add a new and vigorous member to the body of the University, itself a primary organ for the fostering of the spiritual and intellectual life of the whole body of Christian Englishmen. And surely, if our hearts are not cold or our imaginations dull, we shall find in the various gifts and various labours of these our own brethren some help towards recognising that high tasks indeed are laid on the members of an English College, and that the promise of bringing forth blessing to their

own and later generations is assured to them in so far
as they are faithful to the high ideal which the silent
teaching of this Chapel holds up to them. Is it
indeed for mere personal aims, worthy or unworthy,
that we come up here, that we sojourn here for the
few years during which we are learning (or making
believe to learn) the knowledge that is to fit us for
the duties and responsibilities of life? or again is it
for mere personal aims, worthy or unworthy, that we
make our home here in later years? To men who
follow such aims alone, be they idle or laborious,
disorderly or respectable, churlish or companionable,
arrogant or humble, St Paul's language to the Ephesians must of course seem unpractical trifling. Too
often indeed we all of us speak and act as though we
made the same assumption. But in our heart of hearts
we know that all human fellowship, nay all our single
individual life so far as it deserves to be called
human, rests at last on some such basis as St Paul
has here made known. Now, far more than three
centuries ago, in spite of all changes of outward circumstance and inner mind, his language is lit up and
enforced by the needs and aspirations of the time.
Now, more than ever, the members of an ancient and
historic College like ours are warned against forgetting
that they are living stones in a building which, whatever other purposes it may serve, was designed
through all good purposes to be for ever growing into
a holy temple in the Lord.

THE SENSE AND SERVICE OF MEMBERSHIP
THE MEASURE OF TRUE SOUNDNESS IN
THE BODY.

A SERMON PREACHED IN WESTMINSTER ABBEY AT
BISHOP WESTCOTT'S CONSECRATION, ON THE
FESTIVAL OF ST PHILIP AND ST JAMES, 1890.

EPHESIANS iv. 12, 13.

For the perfecting of the saints unto the work of ministering,
unto the building up of the body of Christ; till we
all attain unto the unity of the faith and of the know-
ledge of the Son of God.

THESE words are spoken to us out of the past,
a past which is in one sense becoming ever more
remote.   Already the nineteenth of the centuries
which are reckoned from the coming of Christ our
Lord is drawing perceptibly near to its end.   The
long interval which actually separates us from the
Apostolic age grows unremittingly longer; while the
sense of distance gains steadily in force with the
knowledge that the human race, within and without

Christendom, is setting forth on new and untrodden ways.

Yet this remoteness of time and of circumstance is swallowed up in a greater nearness. It is hardly too bold to say that through all these centuries no generation of Christians has had the Apostolic writings so nigh to them as our own. That instinctive turning to the primary deposit of Christian truth, which has often been noticed as an accompaniment of times of religious convulsion and perplexity, could hardly fail to be called forth to an unwonted degree by these later days. Other influences have been at work in the same direction with perhaps equal power. The study of the New Testament by professed students has been pursued for many years with increased carefulness, circumspection, and regard for evidence. What is more important still, the Apostolic epistles have been gaining immeasurably in freshness and felt reality by the growing anxiety to read them in the light of the personal and historical circumstances out of which they sprang. With good reason Christian men have looked to them for present help, true though it be that they belong to a single age, and to peculiar conjunctures of outward and inward events. For that was indeed a chosen period in the world's history ; and they whose words have been thus handed down for our instruction were chosen agents in the unique spiritual revolution which was then accomplished. Not a Divine enlightenment alone, but also a Divine ordering of the meeting and parting streams of human affairs, enabled epistles called forth by immediate needs to become a perpetual fountain of light; whether through teachings that in the letter were temporary, and therefore would call for varying embodiments of their spirit according to varying conditions, or through the setting forth of verities that by the very nature of their subject-matter are incapable of change.

Among the books of the New Testament the Epistle to the Ephesians in particular has been of late years drawing to itself the earnest attention of many. Enigmatic as might be its language under this or that head, they have felt that it gave promise of at least a partial answer to some anxious perplexities of this present time, and of both sanction and guidance to some of its highest aspirations. It holds in truth a peculiar position among St Paul's epistles; and not in his epistles alone, but in the drama of his distinctive mission. No other writing of his is so little affected in shape or scope by temporary conditions of place or person. It is the harmonious outpouring of thoughts that had long been cherished, but had not as yet found right and profitable opportunity for full utterance; thoughts that doubtless had grown and ripened while they lay unspoken, and now had been kindled afresh by the conjuncture which had at length been reached in the

Divine ordering of events ; for now, after weary years
of struggle and anxiety, what St Paul recognised as
sure pledges for the essential unity and essential
universality of the Church of Christ had been visibly
bestowed from on high.

Both St Paul's character and his work are griev-
ously misjudged when they are interpreted exclusively
by his zealous championship of Gentile liberties.
This fidelity to the special trust which he had received was balanced by an anxiety to avert a breach
between the Christians of Palestine, for whom the
Law remained binding while the Temple was still
standing, and the Gentile Christians of other lands ;
to promote kindly recognition on the one side and
brotherly help on the other. Such a breach, he
doubtless felt, would have cut Gentile Christianity
away from its Divinely prepared base, and sent it
adrift as a new religion founded by himself.

Already in the Epistle to the Romans we find
the two great sections of mankind ranged carefully
on equal terms for condemnation and for salvation.
St Paul's bitter heartache at his brethren's unbelief
is quenched in his conviction that the gifts and the
calling of God are without repentance, and in his
faith in the riches of wisdom whereby God would
make a way for His mercy at last. And then, looking in the face the more than possibility of death
in the intended visit to Jerusalem which his plans
for the preservation of unity required, he uses words

of singular impressiveness to convey to the Romans the joy with which he would afterwards come among them, should he escape with his life. We all know by what an unexpected way God brought him to Rome at last, and that with the purpose of his visit to Jerusalem long accomplished.

To this new vantage-ground St Paul had attained when he wrote the Epistle to the Ephesians. He wrote in the thankful sense that, first, the dreaded breach had been averted, and then that, through his having now been permitted to join in fellowship and work with the Christians of Rome, the Gospel to the Gentiles had in the person of its chosen representative obtained a footing in the imperial city, the centre of civilised mankind, and thus received, as it were, a pledge of a world-wide destiny.

The foundation of the teaching now poured forth by the Apostle to the beloved Ephesian Church of his own founding, and doubtless to other Churches of the same region, is laid in high mysteries of theology, the eternal purpose according to which God unrolled the course of the ages, with the coming of Jesus as Christ as their central event, and the summing up of all heavenly and earthly things in Him. That universal primacy of being ascribed to Him suggests His Headship in relation to the Church as His Body. Presently unity is ascribed to the Church from another side; not indeed a unity such as was sought after in later centuries, the unity of many separate Churches, but the unity created by the abolition of the middle wall of partition between Jew and Gentile in the new Christian society, a unity answering to the sum of mankind. Thus the Church was the visible symbol of the newly revealed largeness of God's purposes towards the human race, as well as the primary instrument for carrying them into effect. Its very existence, it seems to be hinted in the doxology which closes this part of the Epistle, was a warrant for believing that God's whole counsel was not even yet made known.

From this doxology St Paul passes at once to the precepts of right living which he founds on the loftiness of the Christian calling. The great passage which gathers up seven unities of Christian faith and religion is but accessory to the exhortation to "give diligence to keep the unity of the Spirit in the bond of peace"; in other words, to maintain earnestly the moral and spiritual basis of true Church membership. Then follows the correlative truth involved in Church membership, the place of the individual in the community. He is not to be lost in the community, as in so many societies of the ancient world. His individuality is not to be smoothed away and treated as some capricious blemish of nature. Rather it is to determine the character of his service. "But to each one of us"—the words are studiously emphatic— "to each one of us was given the grace according to the measure of the gift of Christ." Already St Paul has spoken of his own unique function of Apostle to the Gentiles as itself a "grace", a special gift of God bestowed upon him for the sake of the Gentiles ; and now he claims the same Divine origin for the particular function of service which each member of the body was to render to the body or its other members. Then, with free adaptation of words from the Psalter, he points to the ascended Lord as the Giver of gifts "to men", and after a short digression applies them to certain typical classes of "gifts to men", gifts intended for the good of men. Some of the gifts which Christ bestowed from on high were apostles, and some prophets,—the two types of exceptional and temporary functions ; and some evangelists, and some pastors and teachers,—two corresponding types of ordinary and permanent functions. Here St Paul breaks off his list of examples. In other epistles he classes with these as functions of service to be rendered by individual members of a Church works of a less definite and official character, while he treats all alike as so many different functions of Church membership. And so what is expressly said here of the men exercising the highest functions, the functions of Christian teaching, was doubtless meant to be believed for all functions alike ; that the purpose for which God "gave" them was "the perfecting of the saints unto a work of ministering, unto the building up of the body of Christ."

The perfecting here spoken of is chiefly the training of stunted powers or organs into their proper activity. It is a process of culture and development, but not with the man himself for its ideal end. Its end is "a work of ministering", some form of service to be rendered to others. For ministering is the one universal function of all "saints", all individual members of the Church, the common element in all functions.

But this various perfecting of the individual members for their several works of ministering had a single end beyond itself, even "the building of the body of Christ". The body of Christ was there already, but it was ever needing to be more and more "built", to be "compacted" in constant renewal in such wise as best to aid the flow of life from "the Head" through "every part", and make provision for a ceaseless "growth".

But beyond the long process St Paul contemplates the end, "till we all attain unto the unity of the faith and of the knowledge of the Son of God." Till all have attained this unity, the unity which governs life and thought when, first, the faith of the Son of God, and then the learning of what is wrapped up in that faith, are lifting them out of distraction, the building of the body of Christ must go on, the perfecting of its several members for a work of ministering must be the aim of its wisest members.

Such is the vision of the Church in which St Paul saw the appointed instrument for the fulfilment of his own best hopes for mankind, and which he desired to bequeath to his most cherished converts, that it might expand their faith and uplift the purpose of their lives. Can we now say that this vision has been clearly present to the minds of even the leaders of the Church through the intervening centuries? Is it not rather in no small degree one of those truths which the new reading of the Bible by the light of new questionings is now causing to be newly discerned? Can it be doubted that from an early time a disproportion grew up among men's various thoughts concerning the Church, so that St Paul's fundamental teaching concerning it receded into the background, becoming little more than a single conventional item of Christian ethics? Such a change in the proportion observed in thought would be the natural, almost the inevitable, outcome of the corresponding change in the proportion observed in actual policy and practice. It is easy to understand how the most pressing difficulties and dangers of the several Churches would come to be met with the most obviously compendious and effective resources, without adequate regard to the less obtrusive and more delicate yet also more vital elements of Church life. In a word, in carrying out the necessary work of building itself up as a corporation, the Church would have needed rare and far-seeing wisdom indeed to save it from unconsciously giving insufficient heed to building itself up as a true body.

Whatever the truth may be respecting the forces that were at work in those ancient days which still exercise so subtle and manifold a power over the minds and ways of Christians, the present state of things is not less the result of other influences belonging to far later centuries. Thus much at least is too sadly evident that, be the causes what they may, St Paul's teaching, which we have been considering to-day, obtains but a secondary part in both the theory and the practice of our Church membership. And if so, can we desire a better ground for hope and consolation than the fact that this mighty resource still cries out to be tried, a resource which by its very nature proclaims its conformity with all that is most full of life within the Churches of Christendom, and with the purest among the aspirations of the uneasy multitude who as yet refuse the fellowship of the Gospel?

On so vast a theme it would be unbecoming here to go beyond the barest suggestion of some general lines of thought. The most obvious need of all is the need of a conscious and joyful sense of membership as taught by St Paul, its dignity and its responsibilities, to be felt by men, women, and children, in every position and of every degree. Were this sense present in many, did many feel it imparting an unimagined life to every Holy Communion, and receiving back an unimagined life in double measure, it would readily find modes of expressing itself in

individual and social action; and in due time more
fixed and systematic forms of service would come
into use, while the service of each lesser unity would
go to make up the service of some greater unity in
a manifold order. But it is in the widest sphere that
this sense of membership, and this practice of it,
would perhaps be most powerful for good. Did sin-
cere Christians habitually recognise that they were
united not merely by a common faith, but by membership of one world-wide society built upon that
faith, they could hardly be content with a fitful and
trifling use of their collective responsibilities to other
men.

The experience of the last few years has shown
how little salutary force could permanently be looked
for in what is called a Christian world, a realm of
habit and language sustained of late for the most part
by vague and aimless convention, though permeated
by Christian sentiment, and partly derived in the first
instance from Christian traditions. For now, helped
by the right and wise tolerance which Christians have
been learning to practise, many who have lost their
Christian faith, or grown up in estrangement from it,
are relinquishing usages in which it is expressed or
presupposed. A yet graver fact is the increasing ac-
quiescence of Christian households in similar licence
for themselves. And these are but tokens and ready
examples of a chaotic condition which is spreading
deeply under the surface of society. Remedies might

no doubt be found without going beyond the accustomed lines. The press, the pulpit, the lecture-room, the school, the home, may all afford opportunities for wholesome and temperate guidance. But what we have to deal with is not a teaching, such as might be encountered by another teaching. It is a confused and disorganised state, affecting to a greater or less degree the whole inward being of men, the whole range of their conduct. Here the one entirely fitting corrective must surely be looked for in the harmonious and effectual working of a common life, inspired by a common faith ; even the common life and common faith of a community of men whose eyes have been opened to the reality and claims of the fellowship which embraces them.

But again, though this corrective action of the Church as a community is what is most evidently invited by present necessities, we can never forget that it is but one side of its positive mission of bringing home to all mankind the light and the life of which it has been permitted itself to partake. Here the Apostolic word transcends our narrow horizon. We can but rest on the assurance that the universal mission of the Church springs from the same counsels as the universality of the redemption.

Doubtless it may be feared by some that the office which has seemed to be marked out for the Church as a community by its Apostolic credentials is one that could not in practice be exercised without

danger to the spiritual liberties of mankind. The
yoke of petty religious communities, where such have
existed, has sometimes been undeniably heavy in
former days, and the yoke of more powerful religious
communities might be regarded as likely to be hereafter found yet heavier. Some again might doubt
whether the sphere thus assigned to the Church as a
community is not altogether wider than the region of
human nature with which it is naturally and properly
conversant. The answer to both these grave doubts
is given implicitly by the breadth of aim and interest
which a Church taught by the Apostles must needs
claim for itself. The story of those small communities of like-minded men, possessed by a dark theory
of God's dealings with men, and of the kind of service
which He requires of them, can tell us little of what
may be expected from large and composite communities of the future, enlightened by those riper conceptions of the province of religion which have been
granted to these later times. Through the same
better teaching we have come to learn that the rightful province of the Church can be no narrower than
the entire world of humanity, because God in Christ
has claimed for His kingdom all things human
except the evil that corrupts them, has included all
things in the range of service well pleasing to Himself, and has set His special seal of recognition on the
service rendered to mankind. Nor is it otherwise
with the ideal which a Church should hold up to its

members and to those without ; for the true Christian life has no special or limited type, being in very deed the true human life, seen in relation to the true Lord and Saviour of man's whole being.

If it is true that the essential relations of life and service between the members of a Church one with another, or of each with the whole, have been obscured by the greater permanence and definiteness of what we are accustomed to call its organisation, yet a reviving sense of their true purport, leading the way to temperate effort to put it in practice, need involve no real breach with the past, no subversion of long venerated order. All true progress in the future must be conditioned by an intelligent use, not of the Apostolic writings alone, but of the varied stores of experience with which the Church of Christ has been enriched in each successive period of its long and changeful existence. On the other hand it could hardly be that a revival of varied corporate service, in which the members at large had their several parts, could fail to make itself felt in that province of service which belongs to organisation. Sooner or later none could be blind to the imperfection, the weakness, the barren divorce from sustaining sympathies, which must cling to an organisation in which the greater part of the members of the community have no personal share.

Thoughts akin to these must surely be present

to the minds of many worshippers in this ancient house of God to-day. We are encompassed by the walls and treasured memorials which repeat to hearing ears what noble works the Lord God of our fathers has done in their days and in the old time before them. In a sanctuary thus doubly hallowed, can we believe that in the time to come He will leave this Church and "kingly commonwealth of England" unblessed with the full richness of those "gifts" of His "to men," all pointing to that one gift of the Son of His love out of which they flow? Uplifted and yet more humbled by those memories, dare we doubt that, save through our own faithlessness or sinful shortcomings, it will in one way or another be granted to this our ancestral community to heal the sorest breaches of our nation, to learn and to teach the way of inward and of outward peace?

But if these voices from our own English past give response to the message which has been speaking to us from the height of the Apostolic age, the occasion which gathers us together as one congregation has another concordant voice of its own. We are met together from north and from south, from the old Northumbrian diocese and the central capital of the realm and many a scattered parish, to join in the act of worship by which a Chief Pastor of the Church is to be hallowed for his office to-day; for the office which, more than any other, links past and present visibly together; the office which, varying in prerogatives and in sphere of action from age to age, is now more perhaps than ever before the organ of active unity, the chief power by which all scattered powers that make for building up are drawn forth and directed.

In commending him now to your prayers, I find my lips sealed by a sacred friendship of forty years from speaking as I might otherwise perhaps have desired to do. But in truth there can be little need that a single voice should attempt to utter what is already in the mind of thousands. Yet a few words must be ventured on for the sake of others. One who has laboured unceasingly to bring his countrymen face to face with the New Testament Scriptures ; one for whom Christian truth is the realm of light from which alone the dwellers on earth receive whatever power they have to read the riddle of the world or choose their own steps aright ; one to whom the Christian society is almost as a watchword, and who hears in every social distress of the times a cry for the help which only a social interpretation of the Gospel can give ; such a one assuredly will not fail to find channels by which these and other like " gifts " from the ascended Giver may flow forth for the common good.

Under these auspices he goes forth to carry forward the enterprise which has dropped from the hands of the cherished friend, united with him as in a common work and purpose so as the object of reverent love and trustful hope. There must be many present here to-day whose recollections of the twin day eleven years ago are full of the echoes of some of the words then spoken from this pulpit. What other last words could speak to us now with so grateful a sacredness?

The pilgrims' psalm which was then made to guide our thoughts "brings before us," we heard, "*the grace and the glory* of sacrifice, of service, of progress, where God alone, the Lord of Hosts, is the source and the strength and the end of effort......*The Lord God is a sun* to illuminate *and a shield* to protect. In the pilgrimage of worship that which is personal becomes social. The trust of the believer passes into the trust of the Church. The expectation of one is fulfilled in the joy of all." "There must be in the outward life," we were finally reminded, "checks, lonelinesses, defects. We cannot always keep at the level of our loftiest thoughts. But for the soul which offers itself to God, which accepts—because it is His will—the burden of command, which claims—because it is His promise—the spirit of counsel and the spirit of prophecy, the words shall be fulfilled through the discipline of disappointment and the joy of sacrifice, *from strength to strength.*

"*O Lord God of Hosts, blessed is the man that putteth his trust in Thee.*"*

---

* *From strength to strength:* a Sermon preached...at the consecration of J. B. Lightfoot...by B. F. Westcott..., 1879 and 1890, pp. 3, 18.

APPENDIX.

THE DECORATION* OF THE EMMANUEL COLLEGE CHAPEL.

THE subjects of the windows of the Chapel, from East to West, are first theologians representative of the Early and Middle Ages and of the two earliest stages of the English Reformation, and then theologians educated at Emmanuel College. The windows on the North side commemorate services rendered chiefly to the organisation of institutions and to systematic theology : the windows on the South side commemorate services rendered chiefly to inward life and thought and to speculative theology.

NORTH SIDE	SOUTH SIDE
FIRST WINDOW	*FIRST WINDOW*
EARLY AND MIDDLE AGES	*EARLY AND MIDDLE AGES*
AUGUSTINUS	ORIGENES
ANSELMUS	JOANNES SCOTUS ERIUGENA
SECOND WINDOW	*SECOND WINDOW*
THE ENGLISH REFORMATION	*THE ENGLISH REFORMATION*
JOHN FISHER	JOHN COLET
THOMAS CRANMER	WILLIAM TINDALE

* This decoration was carried out in 1884 at the time of the College Tercentenary in accordance with a scheme suggested by Dr Hort. The description printed above was drawn up by him for the account of the Tercentenary Festival published the same year.

NORTH SIDE	SOUTH SIDE

THIRD WINDOW — *THIRD WINDOW*

THEOLOGIANS EDUCATED AT EMMANUEL COLLEGE — *THEOLOGIANS EDUCATED AT EMMANUEL COLLEGE*

LAURENCE CHADERTON / JOHN HARVARD — BENJAMIN WHICHCOTE / PETER STERRY

FOURTH WINDOW — *FOURTH WINDOW*

THEOLOGIANS EDUCATED AT EMMANUEL COLLEGE — *THEOLOGIANS EDUCATED AT EMMANUEL COLLEGE*

WILLIAM BEDELL / WILLIAM SANCROFT — JOHN SMITH / WILLIAM LAW

The panels of the walls of the Chapel are inscribed according to an arrangement corresponding with the arrangement of the windows. The North and South sides are united by texts inscribed in the panels of the East wall.

NORTH	**EAST WALL**	*SOUTH*
VNVM	SVRSVM CORDA	VNVS
CORPVS		SPIRITVS
IN QVO OMNIS		IN IPSO
AEDIFICATIO CONPACTA		VITA ERAT
CRESCIT IN TEMPLVM		ET VITA ERAT
SANCTVM IN DOMINO		LVX HOMINVM

VOCABITVR NOMEN EIVS EMMANVEL
NOBISCVM DEVS

The narrow panels flanking the East wall contain

NORTH	*SOUTH*
The pastoral staff resting on the cross, with the olive above.	The vine twined around the cross, with the pomegranate above.

The panels between the first and second windows represent the two great reforming Orders of the thirteenth century, the Dominicans and the Franciscans, on the site of

whose Houses in Cambridge the two Elizabethan foundations of Emmanuel and Sidney Sussex College were
established. The last name on each panel is that of a
precursor of the Reformation of the sixteenth century.

The panels between the second and third windows
represent the Revival of Letters and the Sciences relating
to man, and the Revival of the Sciences relating to nature.

The panels between the third and fourth windows
commemorate services rendered by men educated at
Emmanuel College to the Sciences relating to man, and
to the Sciences relating to nature.

NORTH SIDE	SOUTH SIDE
FIRST PANELS	*FIRST PANELS*
ORDO FRATRVM PRAEDICATORVM	ORDO FRATRVM MINORVM
DOMINICUS	FRANCISCUS
THOMAS AQUINAS	BONAVENTURA
ALBERTUS MAGNUS	JOANNES DUNS SCOTUS
HIERONYMUS SAVONAROLA	WILLELMUS OCKHAM
SECOND PANELS	*SECOND PANELS*
INSTAVRATIO SCIENTIARVM NATURALIVM	INSTAVRATIO SCIENTIARVM HVMANARVM
RENÉ DESCARTES	DANTE ALIGHIERI
FRANCIS BACON	PICO DI MIRANDULA
JOHN RAY	JOHANN REUCHLIN
ISAAC NEWTON	DESIDERIUS ERASMUS
THIRD PANELS	*THIRD PANELS*
INQVISITIO NATVRALIS COLLEGII EMMANVELIS	INQVISITIO HVMANA COLLEGII EMMANVELIS
JEREMIAH HORROX	ROGER TWYSDEN
JOHN WALLIS	EDMUND CASTLE
JOHN MARTYN	RALPH CUDWORTH
THOMAS YOUNG	WILLIAM GELL

INDEX OF PASSAGES QUOTED.

OLD TESTAMENT.

NEW TESTAMENT.

302 INDEX.

H. E.   20 .

CAMBRIDGE: PRINTED BY J. & C. F. CLAY, AT THE UNIVERSITY PRESS.

WORKS BY THE LATE

Rev. F. J. A. HORT, D.D., D.C.L., LL.D.

TWO DISSERTATIONS. I. On ΜΟΝΟΓΕΝΗΣ ΘΕΟΣ. In
Scripture and Tradition. II. On the "Constantinopolitan" Creed and other
Eastern Creeds of the Fourth Century. 8vo. 7s. 6d.

THE WAY, THE TRUTH, THE LIFE. The Hulsean
Lectures for 1871. With prefatory note by the Right Rev. the BISHOP OF
DURHAM. Crown 8vo. 6s.

LECTURES ON JUDAISTIC CHRISTIANITY. Crown
8vo. 6s.

PROLEGOMENA TO ST. PAUL'S EPISTLES TO THE
ROMANS AND THE EPHESIANS. Crown 8vo. 6s.

SIX LECTURES ON THE ANTE-NICENE FATHERS.
Crown 8vo. 3s. 6d.

VILLAGE SERMONS PREACHED IN THE PARISH
CHURCH OF ST. IPPOLYTS. Crown 8vo.

THE EARLY HISTORY OF THE ECCLESIA. Crown 8vo.

LIFE AND LETTERS OF FENTON JOHN ANTHONY
HORT, D.D., D.C.L., LL.D., sometime Hulsean Professor and Lady Mar-
garet's Reader in Divinity in the University of Cambridge. By his Son, ARTHUR
FENTON HORT, late Fellow of Trinity College, Cambridge. In 2 vols. With
Portrait. Extra Crown 8vo. 17s. net.

GUARDIAN.—" We have nothing but welcome for this memorial of Dr. Hort's
life. . . . Mr. Hort has succeeded in giving to the world a vivid and striking
picture of his distinguished father, and he is to be congratulated on the manner in
which he has discharged his difficult duties as editor."

THE NEW TESTAMENT IN THE ORIGINAL GREEK.
The Text revised by BROOKE FOSS WESTCOTT, D.D., Bishop of Durham, and
FENTON JOHN ANTHONY HORT, D.D. Vol. I. Text. Crown 8vo. 10s. 6d.
Printed in "Macmillan Greek." 8vo. 10s. net. Vol. II. Introduction and
Appendix. Second Edition. Crown 8vo. 10s. 6d.

THE NEW TESTAMENT IN THE ORIGINAL GREEK.
An Edition for Schools. Pott 8vo., 4s. 6d. Roan, 5s. 6d. Morocco, 6s. 6d.

MACMILLAN AND CO., LTD., LONDON.

3.97.

www.ingramcontent.com/pod-product-compliance
Ingram Content Group UK Ltd.
Pitfield, Milton Keynes, MK11 3LW, UK
UKHW010349140625
459647UK00010B/951